Fundamentals of Riding

Theory and Practice

...ame author

...NG TECHNIQUE IN PICTURES

...ING AND DRESSAGE

Fundamentals of Riding

Theory and Practice

Charles Harris

Fellow of the Institute of the Horse
Fellow of the Association of British Riding Schools
Fellow of the British Horse Society

J. A. Allen

British Library Cataloguing in Publication Data

Harris, Charles, 1915–
    Fundamentals of riding.
    1.   Horsemanship
    I.   Title
    798.2'3   SF309

    ISBN 0–85131–403–1

Reprinted 1986

Published in Great Britain by
J. A. Allen & Company Limited,
1, Lower Grosvenor Place,
Buckingham Palace Road,
London, SW1W 0EL.

Printed in Great Britain

Dedicated to riders, and riding teachers
in search of safer riding,
common-sense horsemanship and equestrian
scholarship.

'. . . Equestrian scholarship is to possess the knowledge and skills to successfully carry out the desired requirements with the minimum of force and effort . . .'

Contents

Acknowledgements

Special thanks and credit for the illustrations goes to Christine Bousfield, whose talent turned my rough sketches into studies of technical merit.

The equestrian maxims liberally displayed throughout the book, are selected from the author's note-books compiled during the past half-century and are included to make this book as practical and as interesting as possible, thereby enhancing its usefulness.

While there is nothing new in classical riding, there is still much to be studied, observed and recorded, and over many years I owe thanks to my riding teachers and friends, whose instruction and encouragement helped to inspire and originate this book, containing 'keys' to the proper understanding and correct practical development of the 'fundamentals of riding'.

I shall always be indebted to Commandants A. Podhajsky and H. Handler, Ober-berieters Lindenbauer, Wahl and Rochowansky of the Spanish Riding School of Vienna; Commandants Licart and St. Andre, Saumur, France; Nuno Oliveira, Portugal; Brig. J. C. Friedberger DSO, DL, Colonels R. B. Sheppard and G. T. Hurrell OBE, JP, Dorian Williams OBE, and Mrs. Lorna Johnstone OBE, with a very special debt of gratitude to Col. V. D. S. Williams OBE, whose unstinting support and generosity made it possible for me to become the first—and only—English rider ever to complete the full three-year graduation course, 1948 to 1951, at the world's last remaining school of classical horsemanship, The Spanish Riding School of Vienna.

Introduction

It is sincerely hoped that this book will serve *as an absorbing introduction* to the most fascinating of all recreational activities, one which exercises mind and body in a way which has no equal—horse riding.

Many books on horse riding contain elaborate and detailed descriptions of how horse and rider should look when mounted, but usually fail to convey in simple language how such excellence is achieved and carried out. It is hoped that these bare essentials, sometimes repeated in a slightly different technical form, and based on the study and practice of classical equitation, will in some small measure contain those elements for a good basic foundation, and be of help to the majority of riders, including those teaching riding, as well as being the starting point for further study and more advanced riding.

In order to alert the less experienced rider, some extremes of horse and rider postural mechanics have been mentioned and illustrated in the interest of horse and rider safety. For example, it is always safer to be well balanced on a firm base of support, i.e., the rider's seat, by being slightly behind the vertical, than perched forward on the crutch/fork, rocking and continually rolling forward on an insecure base of support, using the reins to hang-on with, and placing too much weight incorrectly in the stirrups, with both legs clinging to the sides of the horse well behind the girth. Quite a familiar sight with beginners and novice riders, and the cause of many problems, and accidents.

The more the riding teacher/instructor, and the rider, pursue practical equitation and equestrian scholarship, each lesson and/or ride, should be a new adventure on horseback, stimulating, educational, health giving and fun. When the riding teacher/instructor and rider can analyse and assess the mental and physical qualities of the horse they ride, they will be taking the first steps towards that equestrian ideal—perfection.

The aim and object of this book is an endeavour to provide some sensible guide lines for the study and practice of horsemanship, i.e., to encourage common-sense riding, and the safety of horse and rider.

'. . . Learning in horsemanship teacheth more in one year than experience in twenty-five . . .'

CAUTION Beginners and riders who have had no formal—or limited—riding instruction should ensure that they wear protective head gear, and have lessons in a proper purpose built riding school, enclosed outdoor manege, or properly fenced and enclosed paddock. It is dangerous to be given riding lessons in an open field surrounded by barbed-wire fencing, and/or with the gate(s) left open, and/or with loose horses in the same field.

The Horse

Elementary Mechanics

'... Think, treat the horse as your friend and your rewards will be much greater than treating him as your slave ...'

The Skeleton

Some knowledge of the horse's body is essential if the rider wishes to understand and control his horse. The skeleton forms the framework of the horse, and it is this framework which constitutes good or indifferent conformation. The way the skeleton is put together, and the various angles of the bones of the limbs, combined with the alignment of the spine, are critical factors in connection with the efficiency of the horse as a weight bearer—and in locomotion.

In all the skeleton is made up of approximately 205 bones as follows:

Head/skull		34
Spine/vertebral column		91
Cervical	7	
Dorsal/Thoracic ...	18	
Ribs & sternum ...	37	
Lumbar	6	} 91
Sacral (fused)	5	
Caudal/Coccyx	18	
Fore limbs		40
Hind limbs		40

Where two or more bones meet they form a joint, and irrespective of the movement in each joint, each joint is lubricated, cushioned, and aided by cartilaginous tissue(s) often forming sacs containing the synovial fluid, i.e., joint oil.

The majority of riding problems are caused by one, or both of the following areas in the skeletal assembly. The atlas/axis/occipital joints which govern and control the (correct) head carriage, i.e., lateral and direct head flexion. Also, the area around the 11th and 12th dorsal vertebrae, which if and when overstressed, is the origin and seat of the 'hollow-back', which seriously affects the way the horse moves and controls his body and limbs.

The angles of the different bones in each limb—one to the other—and over the full length of the limb, plays a critical part in the limb efficiency of the horse in motion, all of which adds much interest to the science of equine locomotion, equine mechanics, and equitation in general.

A good guide to skeletal/limb efficiency, is the length of steps in each stride.

In a free walk the horse should overtrack the fore foot imprints, 2 to 4 hoof prints with the hind foot. With training all horses should be able to achieve this. If a horse loses this ability something is wrong, and it is usually in the training and/or riding.

'. . . A good walk is the Mother of equine locomotion, because it frets and disturbs the horse least . . .'

'. . . If when schooling and training a horse you have a mental blockage, go out for a very long ride . . .'

'. . . Equestrian science is trained and organized common-sense . . .'

'. . . Equestrian geometry and equine locomotion are full brothers . . .'

'. . . Do not lose your temper on horseback, it destroys the capacity for rational thought . . .'

'. . . In horsemanship, a light hand is one which is in communication with the horse, without the horse being aware of it . . .'

Note The skeletal joints described are those where bones move/glide one against another, and directly used as an aid in body movement and locomotion, and not those where several bones are 'joined' (ossified) to form a protective shell as in the skull and pelvic girdle.

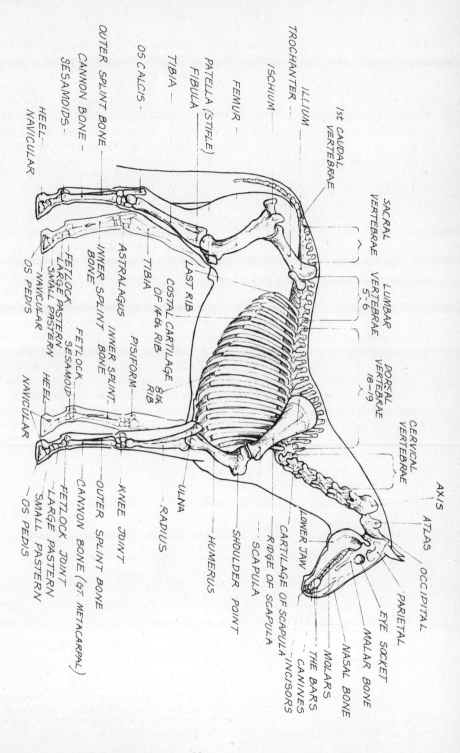

The skeletal system of the horse

ILLIUM

TROCHANTER

ISCHIUM

FEMUR

PATELLA (STIFLE)

FIBULA

TIBIA

OS CALCIS

OUTER SPLINT BONE

CANNON BONE

SESAMOIDS

HEEL

NAVICULAR

1st CAUDAL VERTEBRAE

SACRAL VERTEBRAE

LUMBAR VERTEBRAE 5-6

DORSAL VERTEBRAE 18-19

CERVICAL VERTEBRAE

AXIS

ATLAS

OCCIPITAL

PARIETAL

EYE SOCKET

MALAR BONE

NASAL BONE

MOLARS

THE BARS

CANINES

INCISORS

CARTILAGE OF SCAPULA

RIDGE OF SCAPULA

SCAPULA

SHOULDER POINT

LOWER JAW

HUMERUS

RADIUS

ULNA

KNEE JOINT

OUTER SPLINT BONE

CANNON BONE (Gt. METACARPAL)

FETLOCK JOINT

LARGE PASTERN

SMALL PASTERN

OS PEDIS

NAVICULAR

HEEL

FETLOCK SESAMOID

INNER SPLINT BONE

FETLOCK

LARGE PASTERN

SMALL PASTERN

NAVICULAR

OS PEDIS

INNER SPLINT BONE

ASTRALAGUS

PISIFORM

TIBIA

LAST RIB

COSTAL CARTILAGE OF 14th RIB

8th. RIB

13

The Muscles

The muscles of the horse total in all approximately 540. There are two main muscle groups, the involuntary muscles and the voluntary muscles.

Involuntary muscles

The involuntary muscles form the walls of organs, e.g., the heart, blood vessels, stomach, bowel and bladder.

Voluntary muscles

The voluntary muscles are divided into two main groups—the superficial and the deep muscles.

Superficial muscles These are the outer layers of muscles which protect the vital parts of the body from injury.

Deep muscles In the main these are attached to the skeleton, hold the framework together and cause the limbs to move.

When the horse is in an active and fit condition, his musculature weighs approximately one third of his total body weight. The better the condition of the horse, the more efficiently he can carry the rider/weight, and also perform with relative ease the means of locomotion, at walk, trot, canter, and gallop. There are three main areas where incorrect muscular development can be detrimental to the safety of the horse and rider.

The first group of muscles lie to each side of and underneath the lower part of the neck from under the jowl down into the base of the chest. These muscles can prevent the horse from carrying his head correctly, and in turn can interfere with, and disturb his balance when under the rider.

The second group of muscles are along the top and sides of the horse's back under the saddle. When they are incorrectly developed the horse is unable to retain a convex outline to his back, which in turn develops into, or encourages a hollow back, having a direct effect on the way the horse moves.

The third group of muscles are those which encase the horse's hind quarters, and should in fact be the main motor muscles which drive the horse forward. Unfortunately without the correct work these muscles do not play the part they are supposed to do under the rider, and the horse learns to use the fore hand as a major contributor to impulsion—instead of weight carrying—and this mis-use often causes dragging hind feet, and in some cases dragging fore feet, both interfering with the correct locomotion of the horse.

'. . . Where there is harmony, order and proportion, there is classical equitation . . .'

'. . . Equestrian genius is monitoring intelligent thought with great care . . .'

'. . . In horsemanship—recognise the problem—and you have the solution . . .'

'. . . In equitation speak little about what you have read—but about what you have fully understood . . .'

'. . . If you desire to learn about equestrian science—begin by learning your own language first . . .'

Note The horse's body is made up of various systems. So far we have only touched upon two of them, the skeletal and muscular systems. The other important systems which riders should familiarise themselves with—if they become proud owners of a horse, and/or participate in competitions—are the respiratory, digestive and nervous systems.

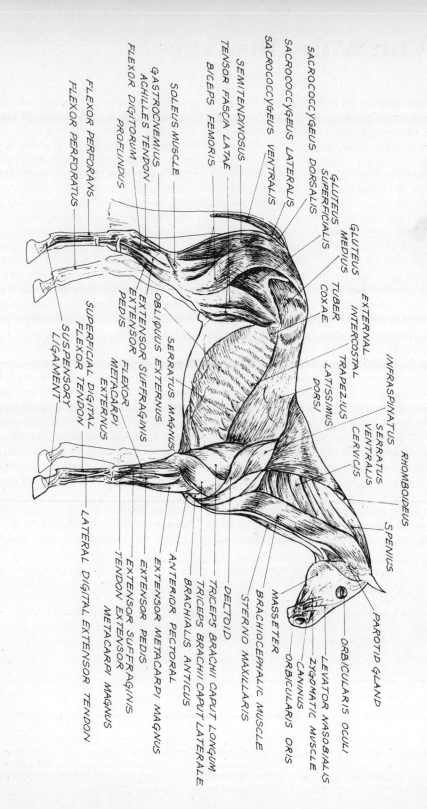

The muscular system of the horse

SACROCOCCYGEUS VENTRALIS
SACROCOCCYGEUS LATERALIS
SACROCOCCYGEUS DORSALIS
SACROCOCCYGEUS SUPERFICIALIS
GLUTEUS MEDIUS
TUBER COXAE
EXTERNAL INTERCOSTAL
TRAPEZIUS
LATISSIMUS DORSI
SERRATUS VENTRALIS CERVICIS
INFRASPINATUS
RHOMBOIDEUS
SPLENIUS
PAROTID GLAND
ORBICULARIS OCULI
LEVATOR NASOBIALIS
ZYGOMATIC MUSCLE
CANINUS
ORBICULARIS ORIS
MASSETER
BRACHIOCEPHALIC MUSCLE
STERNO MAXILLARIS
DELTOID
TRICEPS BRACHII CAPUT LONGUM
TRICEPS BRACHII CAPUT LATERALE
BRACHIALIS ANTICUS
ANTERIOR PECTORAL
EXTENSOR METACARPI MAGNUS
EXTENSOR PEDIS
EXTENSOR SUFFRAGINIS
TENDON EXTENSOR METACARPI MAGNUS
LATERAL DIGITAL EXTENSOR TENDON
SUSPENSORY LIGAMENT
SUPERFICIAL DIGITAL FLEXOR TENDON
FLEXOR METACARPI EXTERNUS
FLEXOR METACARPI EXTERNUS
EXTENSOR PEDIS
OBLIQUUS EXTERNUS
EXTENSOR SUFFRAGINIS
SERRATUS MAGNUS
SOLEUS MUSCLE
GLUTEUS SUPERFICIALIS
SEMITENDINOSUS
TENSOR FASCIA LATAE
BICEPS FEMORIS
GASTROCNEMIUS
ACHILLES TENDON
FLEXOR DIGITORUM PROFUNDUS
FLEXOR PERFORANS
FLEXOR PERFORATUS

15

Points of the Horse

As an important aid to riding it is necessary to learn the terminology used to describe the external points of the horse. Professionals connected with the horse and his activities, e.g., veterinary surgeons, farriers, riding teachers/instructors, horse dealers, and trainers, etc., all use the same terminology to describe and illustrate the points, and/or areas they wish to refer to.

From a riding point of view, it simplifies matters when communicating with the horse, when the teacher asks the pupil/rider to change, or modify the horse's outline, and his way of going. This familiarity with the points of the horse makes the rider more conversant with the understanding and applications of the aids, also the various areas where such aids are required to act. This gives the pupil/rider that extra confidence when in the saddle, leading to higher standards of horsemanship, and more control of the horse.

To learn, and understand the points of the horse, also familiarises the pupil/rider with specific areas of the horse's conformation, all of which must be worked upon, developed, suppled, and balanced, to improve the horse's efficiency, and ensure he becomes a suitable and safe means of transport. This leads to mechanical efficiency in effort and locomotion on the flat, when jumping, and/or when riding across open country, at various speeds and gaits. It is impossible for a horse to move correctly in an upright and supple posture, making light of his tasks, if his limbs—and/or any other part of his body—are too stiff, or too slack, both caused by incorrect types of work, incorrect gait proportions, too much or too little work, and/or lack of condition.

To give the novice rider some idea of what is involved, the horse can be initially divided into three main areas—the hind quarters, the barrel, the fore hand—which the rider must keep co-ordinated to achieve some element of success.

The hind quarters

The hind quarters (rider's legs) should be—but seldom are—the main source of motive power which propels the horse forward when correctly ridden. Unfortunately when incorrectly ridden, the horse must use his fore hand to provide extra propelling power with disturbing results, allowing the hind quarters to become slack.

The barrel

The barrel (rider's weight) is the primary connecting link forming a spring suspension between the horse's hind quarters and fore hand. It acts as the controlling governor, or main control area for keeping the horse fully united, i.e., when correctly developed, keeps the hind quarters and fore hand working in complete harmony with each other.

The fore hand

The fore hand (rider's hands) is the main balancer and steering section of the horse, also it can act as the brake in initial communications. Because of its special physiological and anatomical make-up, it is ideally suited to be the main weight carrier/bearer, the upper part of the limbs forming a spring suspension between the shoulder blades, rib cage, and neck via the muscles and connective tissues.

'. . . Horse riding is made much more complicated by the use of unnecessary jargon . . .'

'. . . A keen rider should observe, reflect and experiment—observation collates the facts, reflection brings them together, and experiment confirms the results . . .'

'. . . A horse which evades and/or resists at one or both ends, causes problems for the rider in the middle . . .'

The points of the horse

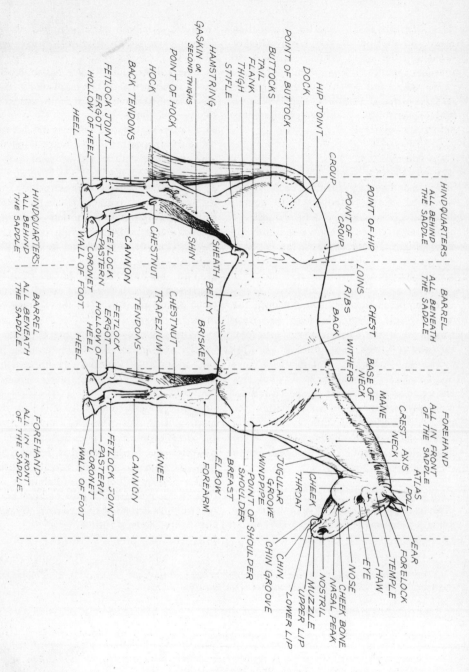

Outline of the Horse

The rider can glean valuable information from the outline of the horse whether standing at the halt, or in motion. If the horse presents a picture of elegance and charm both at the halt, and when moving, then the message is that the horse can stand and move with ease and efficiency for all normal riding activities.

Convex arcs

The overall impression of a trained horse standing and moving correctly, or the young untrained horse standing and moving efficiently, is to give the picture of a series of convex arcs blending one into the other. It denotes that the horse can use himself with maximum efficiency, maximum strength, and staying power.

When fit and correctly muscled-up the horse is able to use his head and neck correctly as a subtle balancing aid, instead of the head and neck being primarily used for locomotion—which is the task of the hind quarters and the hind limbs. Convex arcs ensure fully controlled muscular co-ordination, permitting of variations within the gaits, in speed and length of stride, i.e., regular tempos and rhythms. The convex horse should give the rider a superb feel of controlled horse power.

Concave arcs

With a series of concave, or hollow arcs, the horse is often unable to exert physical control over his own body and his limbs, placing both himself and his rider in jeopardy.

- The hollow backed horse has to expend much more mental and physical energy in an effort to imitate similar gait requirements as the 'round' convex horse.
- The hollow backed horse is much more difficult to control at all speeds, including the walk, trot and canter, and is usually out of control at the gallop.
- The hollow backed horse is unable to use his head and neck correctly as an efficient aid to both balance and locomotion—especially when starting, and when trying to stop, i.e., during changes of speed and in transitions upward, and/or downward.
- The hollow backed horse finds it extremely difficult to reduce speed because he is unable to 'collect' his limbs under his body.
- With a hollow-backed horse, the rider is much safer in an enclosed area, until his outline and his action can be modified so that he is able to move in an improved manner.

Although both lateral sides of the horse—anatomically and physiologically—contain the same number of bones and muscles, it does not necessarily mean that the horse re-acts, or moves evenly and equally well on both sides, or on both reins (directions), or even with symmetrical gaits, unless he is carefully trained and balanced correctly with the 'round' convex outline.

'. . . The important thing in equestrian science, is not so much the gleaning of new facts, but to discover new ways of thinking about existing ones . . .'

'. . . A neglected quality in equitation is the need for a little honest humour, occasionally . . .'

'. . . Good horsemanship has never—ever—been produced by a Committee . . .'

'. . . A horse's muscular and nervous system takes a long time to correctly co-ordinate, so be fair and generous when schooling and riding your horse . . .'

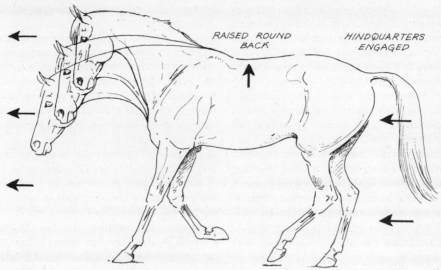

FORWARD THRUST

RAISED ROUND
BACK

HINDQUARTERS
ENGAGED

Series of convex arcs—neck and back. Efficiency in locomotion. Correctly trained horse moving efficiently

MOVEMENT VERTICAL
UP OR DOWN

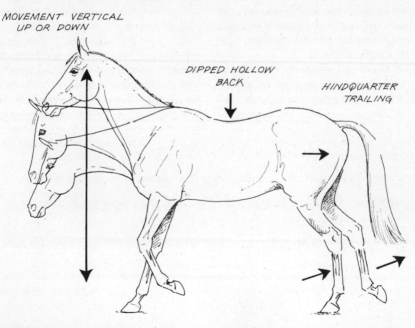

DIPPED HOLLOW
BACK

HINDQUARTER
TRAILING

Series of concave arcs—neck and back. Inefficient locomotion. Incorrectly trained horse moving inefficiently

The Halt

When the horse stands correctly at the halt, with his four limbs, one under each corner of his body outline, or a little within this area, he can stand with the minimum of effort, and move easily into any gait and any direction. A correct halt gives the horse a mechanically efficient posture.

A horse wishing to be disobedient at the halt, also endeavours to take up a similar stance momentarily before 'exploding', for the simple reason that it ensures speed and efficiency in movement, if and when desired. With one or more limbs, i.e., feet which are placed outside of the body rectangle, much more physical effort and postural organisation has to be carried out by the horse to prepare for, and achieve any form of truly balanced movement in connection with locomotion.

This correct posture of 'attention', i.e., upright limb posture with the horse mentally alert and aware of his surroundings, ensures that the horse's spine, especially the lumbar vertebrae are not strained, or under any excessive stress or tension. In this way the horse can carry his head and neck correctly permitting the rider to obtain smooth, light 'airy' gaits and transitions.

At the halt it is possible for the rider to learn, and develop much equestrian tact. This is done while teaching the horse to stand correctly, while the rider is learning to develop those seat, leg and hand aids, i.e., contacts and pressures, which carried out correctly, allows the rider to position the head and neck of the horse in varying degrees of lateral and direct flexion, while at the same time learning how to turn the horse's neck to the right, and/or left. With the ability of 'positioning' the horse's legs where they are wanted, the rider is developing skills which can prevent, and/or eliminate evasions and resistances, including the ability to place/position the horse for desired gymnastic requirements, and physical exercises.

A correct halt is also the best postural stance for horse and rider to commence the early lessons of the rein-back.

As these rider skills develop they will soon become aware of the fact that they can also modify and slightly change the position of the horse's centre of gravity—laterally and horizontally, or both—by simply raising and lowering the head/neck, and/or modifying the action of the hind quarters. Under no circumstances should a rider sit 'slack or loose' as this 'rounded body/shoulder posture' prevents the correct use of the (braced) back, leg and hand actions/applications, whether independently, or in various co-ordinated applications.

When the rider is mounted at the halt, by retaining his correct posture, it will enable him to feel if the horse is standing correctly.

'. . . Equestrian theory is of little consequence without proven practical applications . . .'

'. . . Equestrian art for the beginner is often disturbing, but equestrian science can be very assuring . . .'

'. . . A good seat on horseback is one which absorbs—and does not interfere with—the movement of the horse . . .'

'. . . When schooling horses, tend to cherish their natural instincts, one day it might save your life . . .'

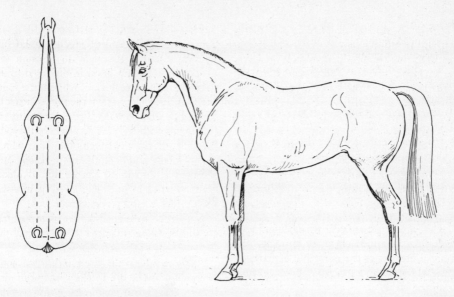

Correct halt. Horse standing efficiently

Incorrect halt. Horse standing inefficiently

21

The Jump

A jump is a lengthened, elevated stride with an extended moment(s) of suspension at trot, canter, and/or gallop.

Walking over a pole/bar on the ground the step/stride is elevated, but seldom lengthened.

When jumping, horses can and do modify their posture to suit:

different speeds at each gait;
different types of obstacles;
different types of terrain;
and when jumping with—or without—a rider.

The slower the speed when jumping—including the approach to the obstacle—the more united must the horse be, demanding more elevation and a greater physical effort from the horse.

The faster the speed when jumping allows the horse to make much more use of his momentum, as an aid to elevation and progression. This in turn demands a little less physical effort from the horse, but much more accuracy, i.e., mental effort.

To jump the horse on various/suitably sized diameter circles, according to his stage of training, encourages both horizontal and lateral flexibility. Obviously the higher the jump the larger the circle, so as not to make the physical demands too severe. A 20 metre diameter circle is quite satisfactory for a single jump—or two at 180°—equally spaced, up to 1 metre in height.

Jumping the horse on straight lines, when correctly united—encourages horizontal flexion only.

No horse should be encouraged to jump with a dipped, and/or hollow back. This causes the horse to carry his head high, and develop a 'ewe' neck. A hollow backed horse has restricted physical and gymnastic ability to jump consistently and accurately.

It is useful for all horses used for general riding purposes to be encouraged to jump different types of small obstacles, up to a maximum of 1 metre in height and width. Such jumping encourages a total limb flexibility, and the stretching of muscles, which is difficult to obtain by any other means.

A 'bascule' is the arched outline of the horse when suspended over the actual obstacle. When correct it should be convex/arched, when incorrect it is hollow/concave.

The horse should be taught to negotiate varied obstacles, first on flat terrain, then on slopes—up and down hill—to develop his balance and dexterity. Finally, he should be worked on different surfaces which offer a good footing.

It would appear that jumping—within the bounds of common-sense and reason—adds interest and enjoyment to the horse's activities.

'. . . In most riding the poetry of motion does exist—cultivate it . . .'

'. . . Most riding faults are the result of what takes place in the saddle . . .'

'. . . A good rider does not confuse equine and human intelligence, and respects both . . .'

'. . . To communicate intelligently with the horse, the languages to be developed are sound and touch—in that order . . .'

'. . . The young horse needs the kind of support you give to an infant, or an invalid . . .'

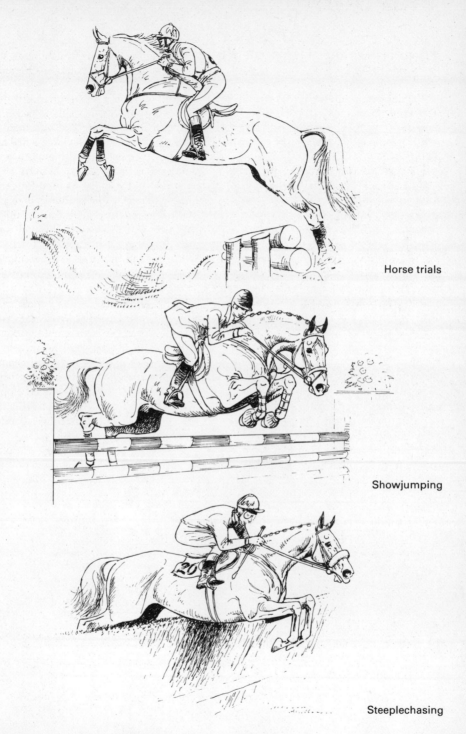

Horse trials

Showjumping

Steeplechasing

When jumping, the horse modifies his posture for different events

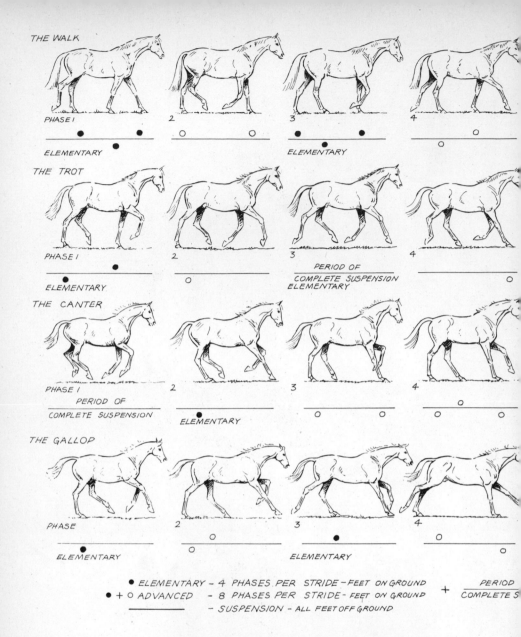

THE WALK

PHASE 1　　2　　3　　4

ELEMENTARY　　ELEMENTARY

THE TROT

PHASE 1　　2　　3　　4

PERIOD OF
COMPLETE SUSPENSION
ELEMENTARY　　ELEMENTARY

THE CANTER

PHASE 1　　2　　3　　4

PERIOD OF
COMPLETE SUSPENSION
ELEMENTARY

THE GALLOP

PHASE　　2　　3　　4

ELEMENTARY　　ELEMENTARY

● ELEMENTARY – 4 PHASES PER STRIDE – FEET ON GROUND　＋　PERIOD
● + ○ ADVANCED – 8 PHASES PER STRIDE – FEET ON GROUND　　　COMPLETE S
——— – SUSPENSION – ALL FEET OFF GROUND

The horse in movement, showing the walk, the trot, the canter and transverse gallop.

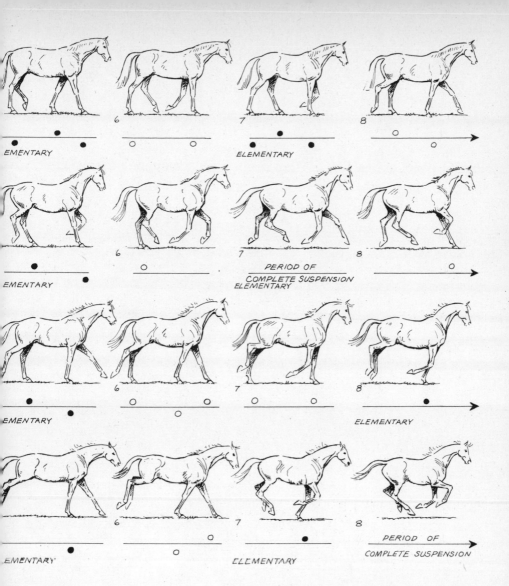

EMENTARY

6 ○ ○ ELEMENTARY 7 ● 8 ○ ○

EMENTARY 6 ○ 7 PERIOD OF COMPLETE SUSPENSION ELEMENTARY 8 ○

EMENTARY 6 ○ ○ 7 ○ ○ 8 ● ELEMENTARY

EMENTARY 6 ○ 7 ● ELEMENTARY 8 PERIOD OF COMPLETE SUSPENSION

25

The Rider

Elementary Mechanics

'. . . The rider's physical posture on horseback lightens or increases the burden for the horse in movement . . .'

The Skeleton

If the rider wishes to control his horse with safety and ease it is essential that he understands something about his own body and how it works.

The rider's skeleton consists of approximately 200 bones, linked together by various types of joints, and forms the framework for the body. It is by the carriage of the skeleton, and its position/posture when on horseback that the rider can be in a good/efficient, or bad/inefficient posture when riding. The way the rider carries himself, and the alignment of his spine are an extremely important adjunct to obtaining the correct rider mechanics in the saddle.

The total number of bones vary at different stages in life. The following number of bones are those of an adult, after some early bones have united and become ossified:

Head/skull—including bone (hyoid)		
at base of tongue		23 bones
Spine/vertebral column		
—Cervical	7 bones	
—Dorsal/thoracic	12 bones	
—Lumbar	5 bones	26 bones
—Sacral (5 fused)	1 bone	
—Coccyx/caudal fused	1 bone	
Ribs and Sternum		25 bones
Upper limbs		64 bones
Lower limbs		62 bones
		Total app. 200 bones

A joint is where two or more bones meet, and however restricted the movement, each joint is lubricated, cushioned, and aided by cartilaginous tissues. Ligaments are the strong cartilaginous tissues which bind bone to bone. Similar tissue forms the sacs containing the synovial fluid, i.e., joint oil.

The majority of riding problems are caused by two main sections of the rider's skeleton. The head and shoulders, i.e., the rounding of the rider's shoulders bringing the carriage of the rider's head and neck forward and downward; and the rounding—stomach collapsing—of the lumbar vertebrae. Either of these two basic faults, prevent the rider from correctly absorbing—and being one—with the movement of the horse. A rider with a rounded—shoulders forward—spinal posture will be projected upward and away from the saddle during equine locomotion.

The numerous degrees of bracing-the-back, i.e., the lumbar vertebrae, in conjunction with an elegant upright posture, is the rider's most important quality, and when fully mastered allows the rider to use the whole of his body smoothly, easily, and efficiently.

'. . . To understand equitation properly, study mechanics, geometry, physiology, anatomy, music, ballet and painting . . .'

'. . . Do not play about with horses—their teeth and hooves have immeasurable impact . . .'

'. . . When it is necessary to subdue a horse, do it with proper physical gymnastics; the whip can frighten both of you . . .'

Note The skeletal joints described are those where bones move/glide one against another, and directly used as an aid in body movement and locomotion, and not those where several bones are 'joined' (ossified) to form a protective shell as in the skull and pelvic girdle.

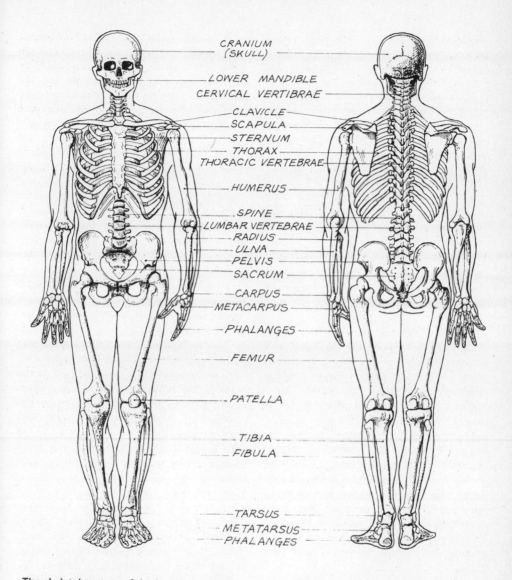

CRANIUM
(SKULL)

LOWER MANDIBLE
CERVICAL VERTIBRAE

CLAVICLE
SCAPULA
STERNUM
THORAX
THORACIC VERTEBRAE

HUMERUS

SPINE
LUMBAR VERTEBRAE
RADIUS
ULNA
PELVIS
SACRUM

CARPUS
METACARPUS

PHALANGES

FEMUR

PATELLA

TIBIA
FIBULA

TARSUS
METATARSUS
PHALANGES

The skeletal system of the human—male

The Muscles

The muscles of the rider total in all approximately 540, the main groups being the involuntary and the voluntary muscles.

Involuntary Muscles
These consist of the heart, blood vessels, stomach, bowel, and bladder.

Voluntary Muscles
These divide into two main groups, superficial and deep muscles.

Superficial muscles Give protection to the vital parts of the body.

Deep muscles In the main, are attached to the skeleton and hold the framework of the body together, in balance, and create the power to move the body and the limbs.

While it is important that the rider should always try to keep his or her body in a reasonably healthy condition, it is not essential for the musculature to be in maximum competition trim. The muscular fitness required for normal riding purposes is simply to maintain the rider in a pleasant, supple, and elegant posture, so that the minimum of effort has to be exerted to remain in balance, and be in harmony with the horse. Until the early part of this century, it was quite normal for doctors to recommend 'gently hacking' for invalids, and those recovering from certain ailments, as a mild form of physiotherapy to activate the internal organs, and improve overall general well-being.

There are two main areas where incorrect muscular development places the rider in a mechanically unsafe posture. The first is around the waist and loin area; and the second is around the shoulder girdle. If those two relevant groups of muscles become slack and loose, the rider will be forced to use the reins for support and balance, while in the saddle.

Also, it is physically impossible to keep correct control of the body from the seat upwards, i.e., the seat being able to absorb the movement of the horse, and the body above the waist cannot remain still and supple to act as a stabiliser to maintain the rider's balance, while at the same time permitting the correct use of the legs, seat, and hands.

Of the two extreme postures in the saddle, it is seldom realised that the slack/loose rider moves about much more in the saddle, than the stiff/rigid rider, and is much more likely to give the horse a sore back, continually rocking and rolling about in the saddle.

To get an idea of the correct posture when in the saddle, the rider should stand upright on the floor, with the feet about 2 feet (60 centimetres) apart, and while keeping the body position upright, very slightly bend both knees—this is the stability and firm balance which the rider should feel, and endeavour to reproduce when in the saddle, a firm, safe posture requiring little effort. Most riders when first put onto the horse are allowed to sit in a 'collapsed' posture, which is allowed to become habitual at walk, and trot, and commences a series of bad riding habits which are extremely difficult to eradicate.

———o○◯○o———

'... Research in practical horsemanship demands direct involvement—and cannot be delegated ...'

'... No horse will have a light mouth for long, if the rider has heavy hands ...'

'... Most riders spend their adult life putting right the bad horsemanship they were taught when they first learned to ride ...'

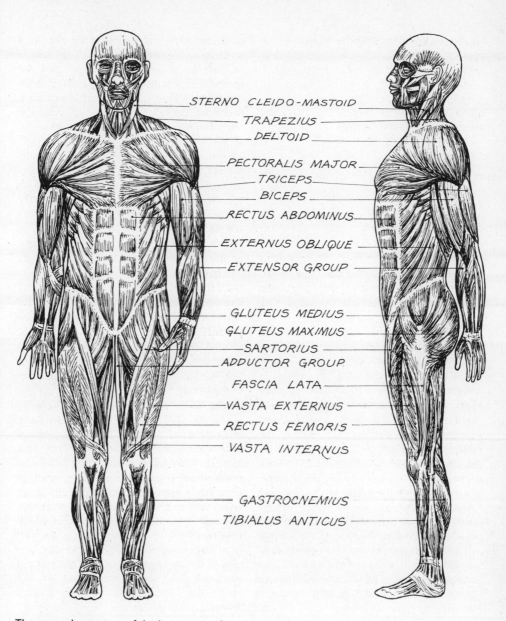

STERNO CLEIDO-MASTOID

TRAPEZIUS

DELTOID

PECTORALIS MAJOR

TRICEPS

BICEPS

RECTUS ABDOMINUS

EXTERNUS OBLIQUE

EXTENSOR GROUP

GLUTEUS MEDIUS

GLUTEUS MAXIMUS

SARTORIUS

ADDUCTOR GROUP

FASCIA LATA

VASTA EXTERNUS

RECTUS FEMORIS

VASTA INTERNUS

GASTROCNEMIUS

TIBIALUS ANTICUS

The muscular system of the human—male

Male and Female Differences

Some general differences between male and female which can affect their riding:

Male	Female
Larger skull	Smaller skull
Shorter neck	Longer neck
Heavier framed skeleton	Lighter framed skeleton
Broader shoulders	Narrower shoulders
Muscular shoulders & arms	Less muscular shoulders & arms
Narrower pelvis	Wider pelvis
Taller pelvis	Shorter pelvis
Heavy boned pelvis	Lighter boned pelvis
Narrower arch between seat bones	Wider arch between seat bones
Angle of head of thigh bone smaller	Angle of head of thigh bone larger
Less flesh on buttocks	More flesh on buttocks
Less flesh on thighs	More flesh on thighs
Knees diverge—'bowed'	Knees converge—'knock'
Upper half of body most fat	Lower half of body most fat
Small breasts—under developed	Full breasts—fully developed
Higher centre of gravity	Lower centre of gravity
Longer limb length	Shorter limb length
Larger feet	Smaller feet
Straight gait	Swinging gait
Maximum muscular power	Two-thirds of male muscular power
Less rapid heart beat	More rapid heart beat
More iron in blood	Less iron in blood
Life expectation lower	Life expectation higher
Active/inventive/aggressive	Passive/receptive/rhythmical
Emotions—vast/steady	Emotions—shallow/transient
Attacks problems	Considers problems/action instinctive
Up to approximately 14 years boys slow in developing	Up to 14 years girls quick in development
Heavier in weight—height for height	Lighter in weight—height for height
Ribcage deeper	Ribcage shallower
Male sex organs. The testicles are contained in the scrotum at the base of crutch/fork. These glands compressed between front arch of saddle and rider's weight can easily be injured, care must be taken to maintain the correct riding posture to minimise accidents & falls.	Female sex organs. Menstrual monthly period pains. In 26 to 28 day cycles, body discharges an unfertilised egg, and app. 2 to 4 ozs of blood. Degree(s) of pain according to well-being—or lack of well-being—of each individual. Sometimes affects the quality/control of horse riding.

Many of these factors are seldom—if ever—considered, and play an important part in the effectiveness of the rider on horseback, especially the lower centre of gravity and deeper seat of the female rider, if and when taught correctly.

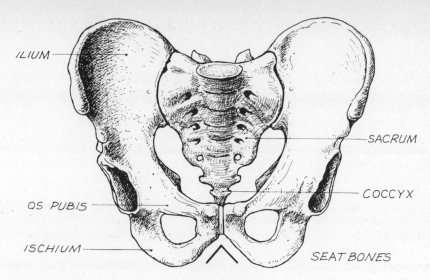

ILIUM

SACRUM

COCCYX

OS PUBIS

ISCHIUM

SEAT BONES

MALE PELVIS
VIEWED FROM FRONT

PUBIC ARCH

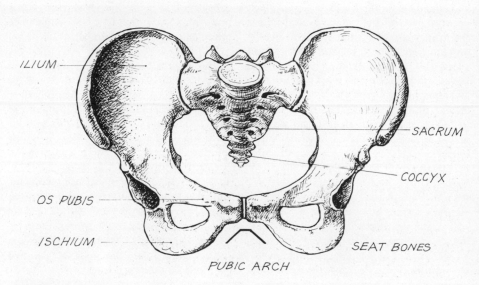

ILIUM

SACRUM

COCCYX

OS PUBIS

ISCHIUM

SEAT BONES

PUBIC ARCH

FEMALE PELVIS

VIEWED FROM FRONT

Human pelvis—male and female. The *deep seat* is more easily obtained by the female rider. Compare the pubic arch and distance between male and female seat bones. It will be seen how much deeper—and with a greater base of support—the female rider is able to embrace the saddle

33

The Rider's Posture

It has always puzzled me, and always seemed strange and quite unnecessary, that the novice rider has to wait till mounted on the horse—in an indefinite posture—before being shown the correct posture prior to mounting. If the rider was given a clear idea of the correct posture while still on the ground, and allowed to feel the stability of this posture without the horse, I am sure much valuable time could be saved with improved standards of balance, safety, and horsemanship.

Dismounted

To familiarise the dismounted rider with correct riding posture, stand upright, elegantly and comfortably, then place the feet evenly about 2 feet (60 centimetres) apart, without moving them backward or forward, and with the body remaining upright, bend the head a little, glance down, and slightly bend the knees till you can just see your toes in front of the knee caps, raise the head again, and settle yourself squarely on both feet. As both feet are evenly placed supporting the body weight, the rider should be able to maintain this easy, comfortable, and upright posture with the minimum of effort for quite long periods of thirty minutes or much longer, and when in the saddle—with the support from the seat—for much longer periods exceeding a couple of hours if necessary.

Mounted

Correct posture in saddle with 'adhesive seat'. This is similar to the posture just described. Body upright, knees slightly bent, a gentle bracing of the loins, and with the feet placed correctly in the stirrups—or without the stirrups—ensures that the rider is in a position/posture which can easily become a part of the horse in movement. The upper part of the rider's body above the waist remains still, upright (modified when jumping), and acts as a 'steady' to ensure the correct use of the rider's weight, legs, and hands.

What generally happens when the beginner first gets onto a horse at the halt, the rider is sometimes placed in a somewhat similar position as just described, but as soon as the horse moves forward, the rider loses his balance—because of the new sensations and having so much to think about—falls forward and/or backward, and having to use the reins for support, originates a series of problems which seldom—if ever—are overcome. While in the riding position on the ground riders could be shown how to maintain their balance while using the lower part of the body to absorb the new and unfamiliar sensations of movement on horseback.

Postural faults.

- Body in front of the vertical, bouncing using reins for support, shoulders rounding causing the feet to slip backward gripping the horse's sides and lifting the rider's seat from the saddle. Rider perched on the crutch/fork limiting any chances of stability when in the saddle. Rider usually loose and slack.
- Body behind the vertical, using reins for support. Rider usually rigid and stiff and with his feet stuck forward assumes a chair seat. Of these two faulty postures, the rider behind the vertical has much more 'saddle contact' and is in the safer of the two positions for horse and rider.

'. . . In horsemanship never lose heart, continually push on, with care and effort you will eventually master your difficulties . . .'

'. . . A good riding instructor must be a psychologist, psychiatrist, politician, lecturer, disciplinarian, handyman, commanding officer, samaritan and missionary . . .'

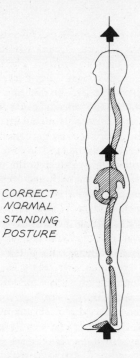

CORRECT
NORMAL
STANDING
POSTURE

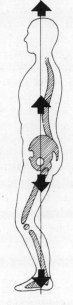

CORRECT
NORMAL
RIDING
POSTURE
(FLEXING OF
KNEES ONLY)

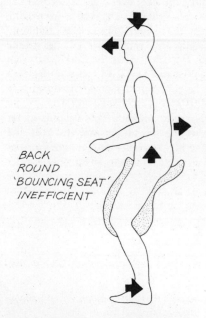

BACK
ROUND
'BOUNCING SEAT'
INEFFICIENT

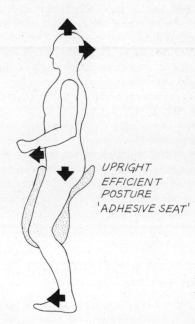

UPRIGHT
EFFICIENT
POSTURE
'ADHESIVE SEAT'

Posture—dismounted and mounted

The Rider's Seat

The rider's seat on the flat encompasses that part of the human anatomy, which without the aid and support of the stirrup irons, is in full contact with the saddle and horse when riding on the flat. The physical contact embodies the internal structures which also help to maintain the rider in the correct balance and posture when on horse-back, i.e., the pelvis, coccyx—varies with individuals—lumbar vertebrae, thighs, and all supporting musculature.

In the main it is the flesh on the rider's buttocks, i.e., the gluteous maximus, and the inner musculature of the thighs—with the musculature kept under strict control, soft, supple, or firm—which provides the essential mechanism, combined with the correct upright posture of the upper part of the body, which allows the rider to correctly absorb the movement of the horse.

The skeletal pressure points on the saddle—under the control of the rider and can be varied—consists of the two seat bones, i.e., the ischial tuberosities, and the base of the tail bone, the coccyx.

The seat is maintained, balanced, and anchored by the pressure of this three point skeletal action on the saddle. The pressure from these three stabilising points can be varied in numerous ways to aid the horse according to his standard of training, and help the rider according to his requirements, i.e., lighter seat, heavier seat, weight to the outer-side, weight to the inner-side, weight a little to the front, weight a little to the rear, etc. There are times in the training of the young horse when the rider's two seat bone contact will suffice, and the tail bone eased. This requires accurate use of the rider's whole body.

The lumbar vertebrae play a critical part in the application and use of the seat, and is the most important—and often neglected—aid in riding. It is the numerous gradations in the scale of bracing-the-back, by the continuous and variable action of the lumbar vertebrae, in conjunction with the pelvic girdle, which ensures maximum efficiency and harmony between horse and rider.

Deep-seated saddles narrow across the waist/twist make sitting in them easy, safe, and comfortable, but such saddles have serious limitations when the horse is in movement. On young, and partly schooled horses—including many almost fully trained dressage horses—they restrict, i.e., lock/fix the rider's body below the waist, and prevent the rider from becoming a part of the horse, e.g., the rider is unable to use his 'seat' as an active aid to modify gait irregularities. On a fully trained dressage horse a deep seated dressage saddle offers one advantage, it tends to lock/fix the rider over one specific point of the horse's spine, but at the same time it prevents that slight—but critical and very important—free movement of the rider's seat.

It is necessary at times to 'ease the weight' on the horse's back. This is not possible when the rider's seat is fixed/locked over one specific spinal pressure point of the horse. Probably one of many reasons why advanced dressage horses and riders seem to have so many gait and transitional problems.

'. . . Reams of equestrian nonsense are published, the diligent rider must search for the pages of equestrian sense . . .'

'. . . Good riding habits and equestrian practice pays excellent dividends—even on the most careless and troublesome horses . . .'

'. . . Once a rider can recognise a correct transition, the time is ripe for studying and practising the use of the braced-back . . .'

Full buttock seat—showing three point pelvic contact with saddle, rider's tail bone (coccyx) and base of each side of pelvis (ischial tuberosities)

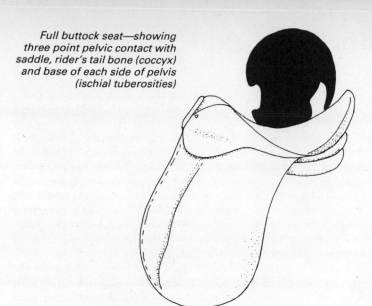

Full buttock seat—showing three-point pelvic contact when rider is sitting upright, or slightly behind the vertical in a more driving/pushing posture. This upright posture gives the rider a vastly larger buttock/thigh contact area with the saddle seat—compare shaded areas. With the fork/crutch seat the rider is often completely out of the saddle

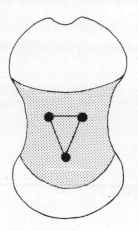

Fork/crutch seat—two-point pelvic contact with saddle when rider is poised in front of the vertical for showjumping, cross-country riding, fast canter and gallop. Additional rider support comes from shortened stirrup length, when the seat must be held up and away from the saddle. With beginners this fork/crutch seat is a sign of bad riding

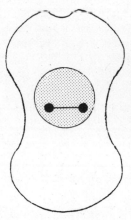

Skeletal pressure points

The Rider's Legs

The rider's legs are very important aids when used correctly, being second to the seat in application and effectiveness. When the legs are used incorrectly they do much harm, not only disturbing the seat but making it physically impossible to maintain a well balanced posture in the saddle.

The legs can be used singly, or both together with varying pressures over a large area on each side of the horse's flanks. On a well trained horse these aid areas are very small indeed, and the movement of the legs negligible.

The action of the legs is most efficient and accurate when the ankle, hip joint, and shoulders are perpendicular over each other, providing the sole of the foot is almost parallel to the ground, or heels just lower than the toes.

The maximum aid area for the correct use of the rider's calves and lower legs, lies between the girth and a perpendicular line dropped down the rear of the saddle flap, i.e, through the horse's centre of motion.

As the aid area of the calf and lower leg becomes smaller with the training of the horse, the rider will find it much easier to remain, and retain the still upright correct posture in the saddle. The normal 'bang-bang-bang-bang' with the heels against the flanks of the horse is totally counter productive, and if carried on over a period of time, i.e., several weeks, the horse will become insensitive to the rider's legs altogether.

Using the legs

Stage 1: free forward movement   During the early stages of training the horse, it is paramount that the action/application of the legs is not overdone, and kept to a minimum. They should initiate the requirement and with subtle application the whip should take over the role of the legs. The whip plays a vital part as a substitute for the legs in early training, and should be applied in areas which encourage free forward movement. Used too far back the whip can cause the horse to buck. The whip can be applied correctly—and with great advantage—to the horse's shoulders, encouraging lightness in front of the saddle, with shoulder freedom, allowing the rider to maintain the correct position with his hands. Gaits; free walk, working (active) trot and canter.

Stage 2: turning; changes of direction; two-track work   The legs, combined with the other natural aids—seat and hands—helps the horse to move correctly parallel to the ground, and in self-carriage, developing further activity from the hind quarters in working and medium gait requirements.

Stage 3: extension and collection   The legs are used with the seat to improve the maximum lengthening of the steps/strides, and the maximum elevation of the steps/strides, all this being achieved with the minimum amount of leg movement.

'... The ideal—and aim in horsemanship—is to endeavour to show that the horse is carrying out his tasks with the minimum of effort and of his own accord...'

'... A difficult horse exposes the rider's qualities—or lack of them—especially when ridden by so-called experts...'

'... To be part of your horse in walk, trot and canter, is an open invitation to the noble art of horsemanship...'

'... Horses have poise just like their riders—efficient or inefficient—the end result depends entirely upon the rider...'

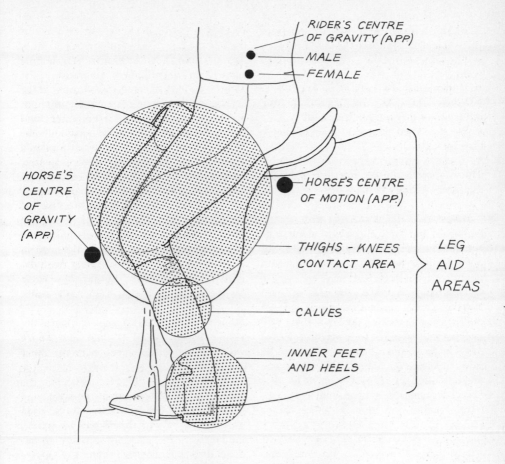

RIDER'S CENTRE
OF GRAVITY (APP)

MALE

FEMALE

HORSE'S
CENTRE
OF
GRAVITY
(APP)

HORSE'S CENTRE
OF MOTION (APP.)

THIGHS - KNEES
CONTACT AREA

LEG
AID
AREAS

CALVES

INNER FEET
AND HEELS

ACTION OF LOWER LEGS AND HEELS
LEGS APPLIED SINGLY OR TOGETHER

- PRESS
- CARESS
- STROKE
- PINCH
- NUDGE
- STRIKE
- KICK

Action of the rider's legs—extreme applications, light to firm

The Rider's Hands

The hands normally refer to the correct use of the whole upper limb, in the following way:

- Shoulders—Act as the datum/fixed point.
- Upper arms—As the main muscle source.
- Fore arms—As the main directing influence—sidewards not backward.
- Wrists—Main source of rein control—give and take.
- Fingers—Supplementary to the wrist action—but should not interfere or hinder the subtle stability of the wrists.

Unless the rider is working with a long/loose rein contact, i.e., weight of the reins alone, there must be a definite, sensitive, but not necessarily identical communication with the horse's mouth on both reins.

The hands can act similarly—or with varying degrees of contact—on both sides of the horse's mouth, i.e., the lower jaw.

The hands assist the body weight, & legs of the rider in keeping the horse 'united'. The rider should never unknowingly loosen one or both reins, even for a moment or two, where he completely abandons the horse, which usually produces evasions and/or resistances, i.e., different effects from those the rider is trying to achieve.

Never, ever, maintain a firm/consistent/pull on both reins for longer than a moment or two, otherwise the horse will learn to lean against the bit and hands of the rider. Under normal riding conditions there should be a genteel smooth 'music', ranging between the lightest and firmer contacts, ever varying the feels and tensions on each rein according to the horse's training, i.e., rider requirements.

The action of the bit in the horse's mouth, should encourage the horse to softly 'chew', thereby encouraging the flow of saliva, keeping the horse's mouth soft, and the bit lubricated.

Using the hands

Stage 1 Riding a young horse—the rider's hands should be carried just low enough to encourage free forward movement, with the rein contact sufficient to give the horse mental and physical confidence in the rider.

Stage 2 Encouraging self carriage—the rider's hands should be held just above wither height—little fingers can rest on top of the withers.

Stage 3 Encourage correct action of the hind quarters—hands, wrists, and fore arms on a line parallel with the ground. This offers guidance, to the increased physical thrust demanded from the horse behind the saddle, i.e., hind quarters.

'. . . There are never two moments alike in equitation—hence the pleasure in riding daily . . .'

'. . . A rider seated on the horse sees more to the front than the horse . . .'

'. . . When in the saddle do not glory in error after error . . .'

'. . . In horsemanship master the simple theory and practice, and you will avoid the problems that plague others . . .'

'. . . In all branches of horsemanship, it is difficult to have success without first having some failures . . .'

'. . . A riding expert is one who knows all the mistakes, and sensibly avoids them . . .'

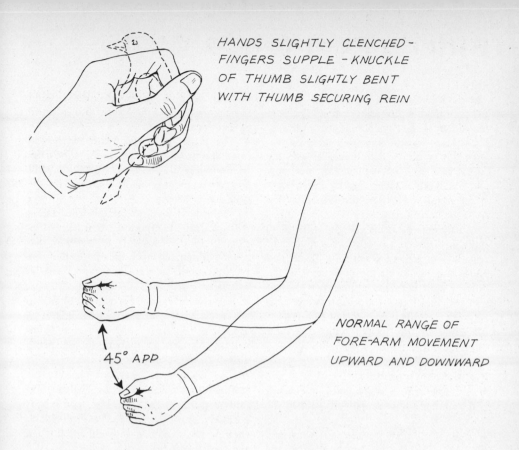

HANDS SLIGHTLY CLENCHED –
FINGERS SUPPLE – KNUCKLE
OF THUMB SLIGHTLY BENT
WITH THUMB SECURING REIN

NORMAL RANGE OF
FORE-ARM MOVEMENT
UPWARD AND DOWNWARD

45° APP

NORMAL RANGE OF WRIST FLEXION IS 45° APP.
FORWARD AND BACKWARD (TOTAL 90°) FROM THE
NORMAL RIDING POSITION

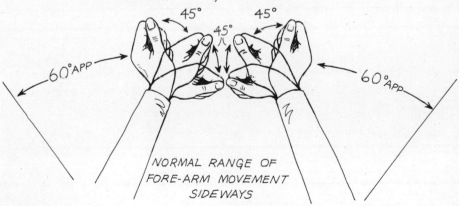

45°   45°
45°

60°APP   60°APP

NORMAL RANGE OF
FORE-ARM MOVEMENT
SIDEWAYS

The rider's hands. Maximum range of movement—most effective range is seldom beyond
these extremes

41

Rider's Position at Walk

The rider's position at walk should demand the minimum of physical exertion. The only movement of the rider should be in the area of the seat—waist to knees—making contact with the saddle, which should absorb the lateral and diagonal sequence of footsteps, and which can be recognised by a very slight sideward roll and forward thrust in the action from the horse's back.

Most riders find this exercise difficult to carry out correctly, because they hold their seat and loins either too loose or too rigid, and endeavour to absorb the movement of the horse's walk with the upper part of their body, rocking it backward and forward. This action is not only ungainly, but disturbs the efficiency of the walk, with the rider interfering with the horse's equilibrium.

Postural requirements

● A supple seat, a supple loin, an elegant, still and upright body posture—above the waist.
● The rider's body between the waist and the knee—i.e., the seat—must maintain the largest absorbing area of contact with the saddle, ensuring the rider is one with the horse.
● The rider's loin and seat must absorb the flowing forward of the lateral and diagonal sequence of footfalls in each stride, while the body above the waist remains upright—and supple—and acts as the datum for the control of the legs and hands.

● The thighs in contact with the largest possible area of the saddle, permits the rider to accurately use the lower legs without in any way lightening, or interfering with the stability of the seat.
● The rider's body above the waist being still and upright without stiffness, allows the rider to use the reins independently of each other without having to resort to them for physical support and balance to remain in the saddle.
● The rider's legs and hands must be free to act as necessary, to guide, to animate, to assist in gait control, to assist in correct figure riding, and assist in applying the balancing aids.
● The walk is an excellent exercise for testing the skill of the rider, i.e., balance and body control, and if carried out and taught correctly to beginners and novice riders, their progress will be greatly enhanced when they commence to trot and canter.
● The horse's walk being the most stable of all the gaits, gives every rider, novice or advanced, the time and opportunity to introduce the most complicated equine gymnastics with the minimum of trouble and complications.

'. . . To understand horsemanship thoroughly—it helps to know all the parts . . .'

'. . . Master the subtleties of the walk variants and you will experience few problems at the faster gaits . . .'

'. . . Equestrian philosophy is a daily constituent for good riding . . .'

'. . . To understand equestrian science it is not necessary to know its history, but it helps . . .'

'. . . Good horsemanship is based upon the understanding of physical science . . .'

'. . . Dear rider—don't just look—please 'observe' . . .'

Note In the rein-back the horse moves backward with diagonal pairs of legs at the speed of walk, i.e., approximately 4 mph (6 kph).

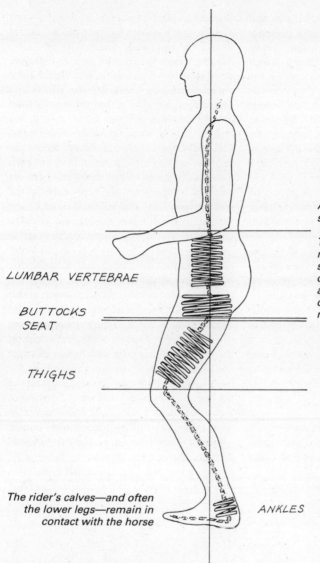

Above the waist, upright and still

There are three areas of the rider's body which can act in a similar way to a coiled compression spring to assist in absorbing the movement/action of the horse—four when the rider uses his stirrups

LUMBAR VERTEBRAE

BUTTOCKS
SEAT

THIGHS

The rider's calves—and often the lower legs—remain in contact with the horse

ANKLES

Rider's main compression spring absorbing elements

Rider's Position at Trot

For the rider there are two trot variants, the rising trot where the rider partially eases his weight from the saddle on alternate steps, and the sitting trot where the rider remains seated all the time.

The rising trot is physically less demanding for the rider—and the horse—when carried out correctly. Carried out badly, it is the cause of many back injuries, and tends to hollow the horse's back. The main advantage for the rider is that it does not jar the rider's spine.

The sitting trot is usually used by school and dressage riders working in an enclosed area, such as a school, manege, and/or dressage arena.

Perhaps the main reason why both the rising and sitting trots are seldom carried out correctly, is because the beginner is often taught the rising trot first, and when doing so is lifted/eased upward away from the saddle by standing up in the stirrup irons, and is allowed to 'fall' back into the saddle at each alternate step. If, and when carried out *correctly* neither trot should jar the horse or rider's spine.

Correct sitting trot posture

The rider's body is held vertical without any stiffness whatsoever, with the loins, seat, and thighs absorbing the up/down/forward action of the horse in trot.

To the onlooker it should appear that the rider is simply sitting still.

Correct rising trot posture

The rider's body is held vertical or just in front of the vertical, not exceeding 2 to 3 degrees. The actual 'rising' from the saddle is minimal, and is achieved by allowing the horse's action to slightly ease the rider's weight from the rear of the buttocks, and not lifting the whole seat from the saddle resulting from standing-up in the stirrups. The greater part of the rider's seat remains in the saddle. To sum-up, the crutch does not move from the saddle, and the rider simply half-eases the rear of his buttocks from the rear of the saddle. There should never be any daylight between the rider's seat and the saddle.

Gait variants

If both the sitting and rising trot—and the transitions from one to the other—are carried out correctly, the rider then has the ability to modify, and/or correct faulty equine locomotion, i.e., irregular tempos and rhythms in the trot variants. It is because many riders are not constant when trotting, i.e., rising too high, leaning too far forward, or falling backward, sometimes with a stiff posture, and other times with a slack body posture—or a combination of all these faults—which prevents them from improving the trot gait, and mastering the several trot variants. If riders were taught the correct sitting trot first, and then the correct rising trot, our standards of horsemanship would be vastly improved.

'... When mounted, never fail to seek knowledge in the riding school, the manege, the paddock, and when moving across country ...'

'... When riding and training young and problem horses, the rider's thighs often act as the main 'cushion' absorbing the rider's weight—not the seat/buttocks ...'

'. . . Most riding instructors are honest, but they vary in their understanding and appreciation ...'

'... Equestrian skills are made up of every-day thought applied to every-day practice ...'

'... If you have a riding problem, ask the horse the question, and carefully study his reply ...'

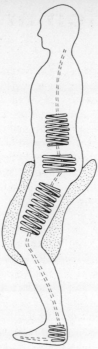

The compression spring action of the lumbar vertebrae is to keep the back slightly braced and body upright

The 'rise/ease' of the rear part of the seat is minimal with the whole of the crutch area remaining on the saddle. The upper part of the body should not be thrown upward and forward lifting the rider completely off the saddle seat

Buttocks/thighs/ankles act as compression coiled springs

Rising trot—buttocks/thighs act as a coiled spring

In sitting trot the main absorbing compression spring is the buttocks, aided by the action of the braced back which can elevate and lighten the seat without losing the full contact with the saddle. If the action of the horse is stiff and jerky the rider can then use the thighs by gently closing them from the top downward, which tends to lighten/ease the seat on the saddle

Primary absorbing compression springs—lumbar vertebrae and buttocks

Secondary absorbing compression spring—if needed—thighs

Ankles should be a last resort if the weight has to be eased from saddle

Sitting trot—loins/buttocks/thighs act as coiled compression springs in combinations to suit trot variants

Rider's Position at Canter

The rider's position at the canter is perhaps the most difficult of all the gaits to master, and carry out satisfactorily. Because of this, few have been able to teach, or describe the action of the rider's seat and body posture with accuracy and sensitivity.

The sequence of seat sensations/actions/feels, varies according to the length of the canter stride, and at each complete stride. *The rider's seat should flow* circumscribing a series of arcs, which form the outline of the lower half of an egg, i.e., looking at the egg from the side.

Sequence of seat sensations at canter

1. *The immediate lowering/sinking of the seat* by slightly relaxing the seat and loins, at one and the same time, and having reached the lowest point . . . .
2. *Floating forward of the seat*, with upright/supple body posture, with a gradual firming of the loins, but not that of the buttocks which remain soft/supple and relaxed. This immediately becomes the basis for, and part of . . .
3. *The gentle floating forward/upward following a 'comfortable concave arc'*, as if the rider's seat was 'stitched to the saddle seat'. This completes the first stride, and without any break into No 1 again, the immediate lowering/sinking of the seat and supple upright body, etc . . .

These three quite separate and distinct sensations/actions/feels, are blended into *one flowing movement*—down/forward/upward

—at every stride of the canter, only being slightly modified to suit the length and/or elevation of the canter stride(s).

At no point in the canter stride—or from one canter stride to the next should the weight of the rider—through the medium of the seat—ease/lift itself upward and away from the saddle. The main fault with the majority of riders at the canter, is rising (as in the trot . . .) or being thrown upward away from the saddle at every stride, then falling back onto the saddle with a thump, to be thrown upward once again, and so on. Obviously this rider activity leads to numerous postural faults, and much discomfort to horse and rider.

The pleasure of riding at the canter is its smooth/regular undulating 'swing', flowing in the saddle without any jarring or concussion whatsoever throughout the whole body.

A good rider should be able to brace his back into any canter variant with ease, and the minimum disturbance to the horse.

Posture Modification

When jumping at the canter on the flat, it is usual for the rider's body to be held slightly braced, and just in front of the vertical, with the seat slightly elevated—and held—just above, and away from the saddle while conforming to the rhythmical flow of the canter. The ideal posture for the average rider is that the rider's centre of gravity should coincide with that of the horse, i.e., being on a vertical line over that of the horse.

'. . . A rider's muscular and nervous system takes a long time to be efficient on horseback, therefore dismounted activity should never be careless . . .'

'. . . Horses the world over are made up of the same constituent parts, but their temperaments vary enormously—and riding applications must be varied to suit their different characters . . .'

'. . . To sit correctly at canter is a joy denied most riders—sitting incorrectly at canter is the cause of many riding problems, and often serious accidents . . .'

1 Thighs remain 'adhesive' on the saddle flaps during the sinking of a supple seat and loins

2 Floating forward of the supple seat (buttocks and loins) always remaining and bottoming on the saddle seat

3 Supple seat and loins slowly rise being pushed upward/forward/ eased by and still remaining in the saddle

This sequence/series of applications are carried out as one smooth, definite continuous curve—stride by stride

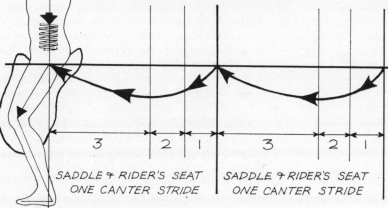

Canter—correct seat never leaving saddle

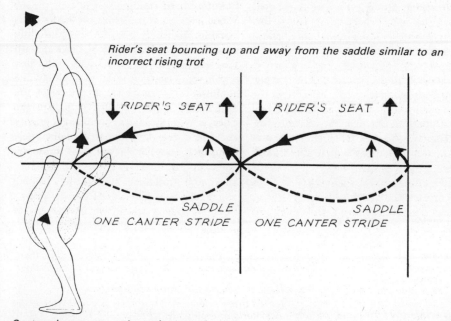

Canter—incorrect seat bouncing out of saddle

Rider's Position at Gallop

The rider's position at the gallop is most efficient when it is modified to suit the various speeds and vagaries of each horse, combined with the skill and ability of the rider. According to the conformation of each horse—while they might well be travelling at the same speed—the gallop differs from horse to horse more than any other gait.

Postural considerations

Average horse/rider	—¼ speed gallop	A horse not trained or fit to gallop correctly, can be extremely difficult to handle/hold. Therefore it is imperative that the ordinary rider does not behave in a reckless manner.
Unfit horse/rider	—½ speed gallop	
	—¾ speed gallop	
	—Full speed gallop	

Rider/Thoroughbred horse	—¼ speed gallop	Riders galloping fit horses also admit to learning every time riding conditions change, and in differing environments.
Fit horse/rider	—½ speed gallop	
	—¾ speed gallop	
	—Full speed gallop	

There are two main considerations riding at differing speeds in gallop. The restraining posture and the balanced posture.

The restraining posture In which the rider tends to lean against the reins in an almost vertical posture, sometimes standing upright, and/or tending to lean backward against the reins when riding short, i.e, stirrup leathers. Rider above or behind centre of motion.

The balanced full speed gallop posture When the rider is seeking maximum effort from the horse, where the horse is given the necessary rein support to maintain his balance for maximum speed/effort. This rein support is usually in a continuous state of flux during the gallop, and becomes more subtle at the stage where the horse is beginning to tire, and tends to wave/wander laterally due to fatigue. Rider over or just behind horse's centre of gravity.

There are also numerous modifications when jumping at the gallop, e.g., eventing, cross country, steeplechasing, point-to-pointing, when the safety of horse and rider is of paramount importance, whether the jumping is at gallop on level or unlevel terrain.

Under these conditions it is safer for the rider to err from the vertical—to behind the vertical—posture, which places the rider over the horse's centre of motion, and not over the horse's centre of gravity.

The true science/art of restraining—or retaining—the horse at gallop, is to prevent 'a completely dead heavy pull' against the horse's mouth—lower jaw—which causes the rider to become rigid/stiff, and physically incapable of applying any change of tension/force to the reins. Even at the point of maximum effort there should always be some slight variant in rein contact, to prevent the horse becoming insensitive to the rider's main means of control—voice and hands.

'. . . The true science and art of equitation is to seize the correct moments . . .'

'. . . A good rider flows or floats when in the saddle, but never—ever—bounces or bumps on the horse's spine . . .'

1 *Restraining posture—rider slightly in front of the vertical some 5 to 10 degrees approximately according to temperament of the horse. Rider may be vertical, or just behind vertical maintaining steady pulls on the reins*

2 *Half-speed posture—rider has weight off horse's loins, and is in a semi-perched posture, approximately 30 to 40 degrees in front of the vertical*

3 *Full speed gallop posture—rider well forward in slightly crouched posture, bringing the rider closer to the horse's centre of gravity, and reducing wind resistance*

Rider's position at gallop. In all gallop postures the rider adjusts his stirrups two to four holes shorter, to suit horse, speed and task

Rider's Posture when Jumping

Posture on level ground

The jump can be considered as an elevated and/or lengthened stride of walk, trot, canter and gallop, during which time the rider can adopt a forward, upright, or behind the vertical posture on the horse which can range forward from the horse's centre of motion to his centre of gravity.

On slopes, up and downhill

Jumping up or downhill places an extra burden on the horse, where the rider has to play an important part, i.e., making it as easy for the horse as possible. Downhill trying to ease the effort of the forehand and forelegs of the horse. Uphill, trying to ease the additional effort of the demands made upon the horse's hindquarters.

Gait speeds

Walk   While maintaining an active walk the rider does not alter his posture in any way whatsoever. Walking (over poles) on the ground has a good effect on the flexion of all the joints in horse's limbs.

Trot   The trot must be held thoroughly united over small obstacles, while the rider can adopt one of two postures. Sitting trot allowing the upper part of the body to come slightly in front of the vertical over the obstacle, or rising trot with a similar in front of vertical poise, over the obstacle.

Canter   The canter must be sustained with just enough impetus coming through the final three strides approaching the jump to ensure that the horse can jump cleanly and efficiently. The rider's posture can be 'seated', or poised in a slightly forward position, above and away from the saddle; there must be no bumping backward/downward onto the saddle at every stride approaching/over/or moving away from the obstacle.

Gallop   Jumping when the horse is galloping demands that every safety first precaution is taken, and it will be seen that in the majority of cases where the type of jumps are continually changing—or the environment changes—i.e., there is an element of doubt, the rider stays close to the horse's centre of motion, i.e., upright or behind the vertical, while giving the horse the freedom to jump the obstacle without hindrance.

'. . . All riders and instructors must be made fully aware of the difference between the horse's centre of gravity and the horse's centre of motion . . .'

'. . . To obtain the best in equine locomotion, the rider must reduce his own body movement to almost nil . . .'

'. . . All horses are born with natural movement—but not all horses are born with good movement . . .'

'. . . Wise horsemen, and horsewomen sort out their problems on the drawing board where no harm can be done—and not when mounted in the riding school, arena, or paddock . . .'

Note   Any jumping posture which is vertical or in front of the vertical should always be maintained with a slight bracing of the back. If the rider collapses his stomach muscles and rounds his shoulders, any evasion, resistance, or 'pecking' of the horse will catapult the rider from the saddle, or make it extremely difficult for the rider to control his body posture in the saddle.

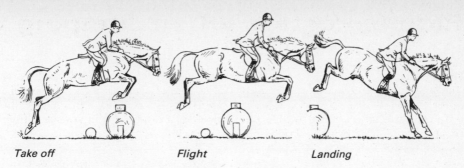

Take off   Flight   Landing

Jumping at canter on level ground. Rider remains still in front of the vertical, some 30 to 40 degrees with the seat just out of the saddle.

Jumping at gallop on varied terrain

1 Rider well forward 40 to 50 degrees in front of the vertical maintaining a smooth definite rein contact

2 Rider in balanced posture 15 to 20 degrees in front of the vertical going well with the horse and not in any way interfering during jump

3 Rider behind the vertical—essential when rider is unsure of the horse, width of obstacle, over water, over drops, wide ditches, before or after obstacle. Also used to ensure the horse gallops on towards, and over the obstacle(s)

Stirrups for all jumping are shortened to suit speed, type of obstacles and terrain, two holes for obstacles up to one metre and then shorter still for higher and varied obstacles, the shortest usually being for steeplechasing and hurdling

51

Horse and Rider

Elementary Mechanics

'... For grandeur and regality there is nothing to compare with the noblesse of horse and rider ...'

Getting into the Saddle

The way the rider gets into the saddle can make or mar a good ride or lesson. Therefore it is essential that mounting should be carried out easily and with the minimum of effort, i.e., correctly, so that neither horse nor rider tries each others patience. A competent assistant should be used whenever necessary, especially with horses which often have a slight problem when being mounted, e.g., a little 'nervy', a cold back, extending their chest when the girths are tightened, etc. If anything untoward has been known to happen during the mounting stage, it is wise to longe the horse for five or six minutes on each rein with saddle correctly fitted.

Before mounting ensure that the saddle and bridle—and boots if fitted—are all correctly adjusted, and the girth(s) is tight enough to prevent the saddle slipping. The stirrup leathers should also be adjusted evenly and to approximate correct length as shown opposite.

Brief guide to mounting

Use the method best suited to the agility of the rider. These instructions are for mounting the horse from the left side, it is advisable for the rider to learn to mount from the right side with the same dexterity.

Mounting facing the rear

1. Take the reins and whip in left hand and place left hand in front of the withers.
2. Turn left stirrup iron clockwise with right hand and place left foot securely in stirrup iron.

3. Turn facing the side of the horse and as close as possible, and place right hand across/holding the waist or rear of the saddle.
4. Lightly spring up, and place right leg clear/over horse and saddle.
5. Right hand lightly supported on the front arch gently sit in saddle.

Mounting facing the front

1. Take the reins and whip in the left hand and place left hand in front of the withers.
2. Place right hand over the pommel/front arch of saddle.
3. Place the left foot securely into the left stirrup iron.
4. Lightly spring up, placing the right leg clear/over horse and saddle.
5. Right hand lightly supported on the front arch, gently sit in saddle.

Mounting block

This can be used to aid both forward or rear facing mounting.

Dismounting

1. Remove both feet from stirrup irons.
2. Place whip/reins into left hand supported on horse's neck.
3. Place right hand on front arch and swing right leg clear of saddle and horse.
4. Allow the body to slide gently/slowly down to the ground.
5. Re-adjust whip and the reins to control horse when holding or leading.
6. Finally ease girth two/three holes and slide stirrup irons to top of leathers.

'. . . In equestrian scholarship there are two forms of intelligence to be considered and co-ordinated—human and equine . . .'

'. . . In horsemanship it is a quality to be modest and humble, but try to avoid making an idiot of yourself . . .'

'. . . The greatest puzzle in equitation is simply not knowing . . .'

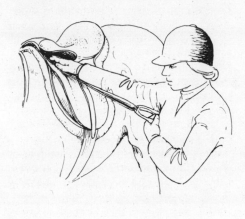

CHECK SADDLERY & STIRRUP IRON LENGTH

MOUNTING-FACING REAR

MOUNTING-FACING FORWARDS

DISMOUNTING

Getting into the saddle—note the left toe is kept clear of the horse

At the Halt

When horse and rider habitually stand incorrectly at the halt—whatever the reason—seeds are sown which must inevitably lead to bad riding, and bad riding habits.

A slack horse and rider are unable to act correctly to normal riding aids, without much ado, a lot of effort, and excessive movement. This behaviour causes riding to become indefinite, less satisfying and unsafe. Standing slack/loose, encourages sluggish/idle gaits causing problems at walk, trot, canter, and especially gallop. In total this all leads up to the horse developing a hollow back and ewe neck, giving the horse minimal control over his limbs, and rider minimal control over the horse.

The stiff horse and stiff rider at halt, usually re-acts quicker and much more definitely, but as with the slack/loose horse and rider, it is at the expense of being 'one with the horse' from the moment of mounting. Both types of horses and riders put far too much effort into moving from the halt, simply because the horse is allowed to stand inefficiently.

Saddlery should be of the *best* available quality—fitted correctly—so that the maximum of comfort is assured for the horse, and maximum equestrian advantage for the rider.

Correct halt—horse and rider

1. The rider should sit comfortably, i.e., easy, elegant, and upright, using the minimum of tension to maintain this correct posture, which gives instant control over the rider's body and that of the horse.

2. The horse must stand correctly over his four limbs, each taking its share of weight bearing, so that he can move off instantly at the request of the rider, both horse and rider moving off in harmony.

3. So that the horse and rider remain in balance, supple and alert, it is essential that both sub-consciously learn to maintain a posture which makes the minimum demand on their musculature. From such a posture at halt, the horse and rider should be able to move into any gait, or gait variant, figure and/or exercise with the minimum of effort.

4. A good halt is the foundation of all intelligent horsemanship, and ensures that 'equine locomotion' commences correctly.

5. A good halt can prevent the rider from falling into many bad habits:

- Moving-off behind the movement of the horse;
- Moving-off in front of the movement of the horse;
- Excessive use of hand/rein aids;
- Excessive use of leg/spur aids;
- Excessive use of body/weight aids.

6. To be one with the horse at the halt—and in movement—demands a certain amount of physical agility combined with mental dexterity, and is only possible when horse and rider are physically and mentally in tune with each other.

'. . . In good riding the whole horse is under the influence of the rider—not just parts of the horse . . .'

'. . . As the horse becomes lighter between hand and leg—normal aid applications begin to pale into insignificance . . .'

'. . . Every horse and rider is different—thank goodness—so there must always be slight variations in the aids to obtain the best possible results . . .'

'. . . For the best results the mind and body of horse and rider must work in total harmony . . .'

'. . . Perfection in horsemanship, is when all the parts work together in unison . . .'

'. . . Invite the horse to carry out your desires—never force him . . .'

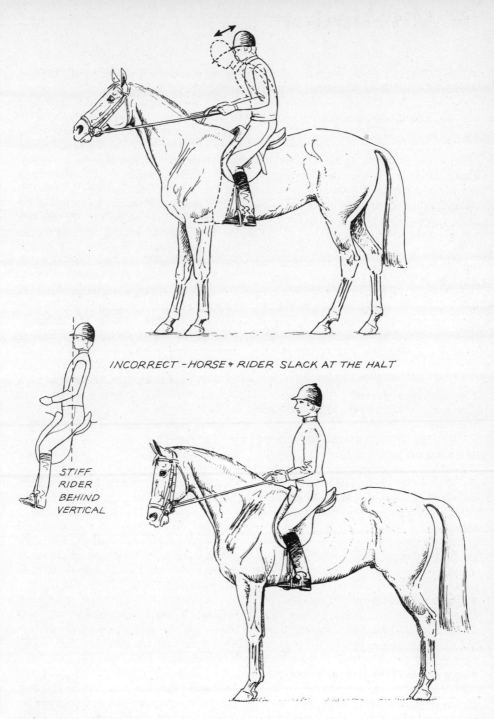

INCORRECT – HORSE & RIDER SLACK AT THE HALT

STIFF
RIDER
BEHIND
VERTICAL

CORRECT – HORSE & RIDER EFFICIENT IN BALANCE / ALERT AT HALT

At the halt

In Movement

To the person able to ride correctly there is no confusion in 'being part of the horse' in movement, i.e., possessing those perceptive and sympathetic responses which constitute good horsemanship.

Unfortunately, many who ride well, i.e., instinctively ride well, make some of the most glaring mistakes when trying to describe the horse and rider in movement, and appear to be completely unaware of some of the simplest aspects of equine locomotion, and equestrian mechanics.

To 'follow' the movement of the horse, implies that the rider is always 'behind' the horse in movement. If the rider wishes to contribute to the efficiency of the horse in movement, it is essential to be 'a part of the horse in movement', not behind, nor in front, but in harmony thereby assisting with impulsion, momentum, and locomotion.

The horse in movement
How does the rider become part of the horse in movement?
1. By using his body posture, weight, and limbs in a manner to improve the stability and balance of horse and rider.
2. Without the correct body posture, the co-ordinated use of the rider's weight, legs and hands will never be consistent, and/or in harmony.

To obtain the correct body posture there are three specific areas which must be consolidated—the seat, the legs and the body above the waist.
● The seat—Embracing the rider's body from waist to knee inclusive, i.e. the actual seat area in full contact with the saddle, and the lumbar vertebrae/the loins acting through the seat. The loins act as a coiled spring absorbing much of the movement of the horse, and also act as a balancer between the upper and lower half of the rider's body.
● The legs—From the knees down (without disturbing the seat) the legs slide backward and forward in contact with the sides of the horse, and can also exert direct/

inward pressure against the horse's flanks—as and when required.
● The body above the waist—The upper half of the body is the datum by which the rider measures and controls the activity of the lower half of the body, i.e., the seat. Because the upper part of the body is kept still, supple, and upright, the rider is able to direct the use of the hands accurately and with minimum force. When the upper half of the body retains its correct posture, the loins and the seat can act as two separate coiled compression springs, to absorb, balance, and vary the seat pressure—*without ever reducing the seat contact area with the saddle.*
3. The rider sitting correctly on horseback during movement, should appear to be quite still/supple/upright, unless he knowingly wishes to use the upper part of the body to implement the seat when trying to overcome a problem, or in the riding of difficult horses.
4. The good rider should be able to place the weight in the following areas of the saddle:
● spread over the full area of the saddle—seat and flaps
● spread over saddle seat only—through the buttocks/light thighs
● spread over the saddle flaps only—firm thighs/light buttocks

To Walk Retain communication with both reins—and apply intermittent increasing pressure with both legs till the walk is established. Then modify aids to maintain gait variant(s).

To Trot Retain communication with both reins—apply intermittent pressure with both legs till the trot is established. Then modify aids to maintain gait variant(s).

To Canter Retain communication with both reins, and at the same time gently lighten the 'leading' foreleg—increase the pressure with both legs, the outer leg a little firmer and slightly further back than the inner leg. Then modify aids to maintain gait variant(s).

In movement. To obtain the best results in transitions and the gaits, the horse's spine should be a series of varying convex/arched curves. Not concave/hollow backed. Hence the importance of teaching the horse a well balanced halt as the key to correct locomotion for the less experienced rider.

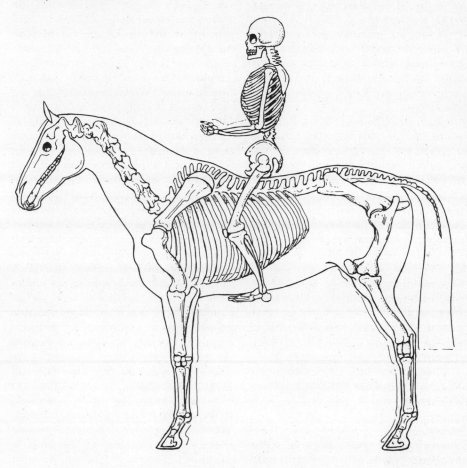

Origin of correct and efficient movement

Note The rider should never lose sight of the fact that when riding the horse, it involves the combined control of approximately 405 bones and 1080 muscles. Horse 205 bones/540 muscles, rider 200 bones/540 muscles.

Communications

Communication when riding commences with the moment of mental and physical contact, which the horse learns to respect and/or fear. It is through the voice, seat, weight, legs and hands—all of which can soothe, comfort, give assurance, and confidence, or can frighten and bully, that the horse quickly learns to recognise, obey, resist, evade and/or ignore.

Natural aids

In order of merit these are the seat, legs and hands. Once the rider has settled himself in the saddle, at no time on horseback, should the correct, and/or required means of communication between horse and rider be broken or terminated, unless specifically desired.

Even when riding on a long or loose rein, the means of communication with the horse should be maintained by the rider's seat and legs.

The seat, legs and hands should always work in harmony; leading, flexing, easing, tensioning, guiding, uniting and controlling the horse with minimal force. The seat, legs and hands should act in their different roles, proportions, and various sequences to encourage and develop the most efficient use of the horse's qualities and faculties—both mental and physical.

The seat

The rider's seat conveys the 'music' of the horse's body to the rider, and by the weight of the seat maintains stability in the saddle, enabling the rider to use the natural aids in their many and varied combinations.

The legs

The thighs are used as a secondary aid—working with and implementing the use of the seat. Without force, and simply by the weight of the rider, the action/application of the thighs can vary the 'weight' dispersal on the saddle. The legs from the knee down, are the means by which the movement, and the positioning of the horse is achieved, with support by the nuances of all the other natural aids.

The hands

The hands are very important riding aids and—except during emergencies—should never be used solely, or primarily, for the purpose of 'hanging on', i.e., to keep the rider in the saddle.

The hands when in action are extremely subtle aids, uniting and directing the forehand, from the forward drive/impulsion created by the hindquarters, so that the horse moves correctly in balance, and harmony, i.e., efficiently.

There is a term often used in equitation of 'lifting the horse'. In the ordinary sense of the term, this is a mechanical and physical impossibility. It is a technical term used in equestrian science, to describe the rider's action of lightening the action/movement of the horse, by closing the legs, bracing the back, and with a varying resistance—not pulling backward on the reins—the rider encourages longer moments of suspension/elevation, step by step, and stride by stride. Sometimes this action is described as a half-halt.

Artificial aids

These are mechanical appliances which are used by riders to enforce their wishes upon the horse, e.g., whips, spurs, martingales, special forms of rein devices, etc. Generally excluded from the list of artificial aids is the snaffle bridle, double bridle, and the fully furnished saddle.

'. . . The voice, six legs, two arms, and two bodies, should suffice for anyone with equestrian ambition . . .'

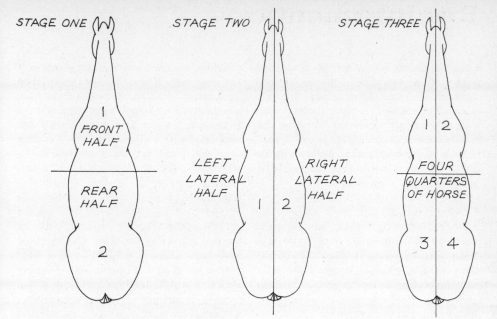

STAGE ONE

1
FRONT
HALF

REAR
HALF

2

STAGE TWO

LEFT
LATERAL
HALF

RIGHT
LATERAL
HALF

1 | 2

STAGE THREE

1 | 2

FOUR
QUARTERS
OF HORSE

3 | 4

Learning to communicate with the horse

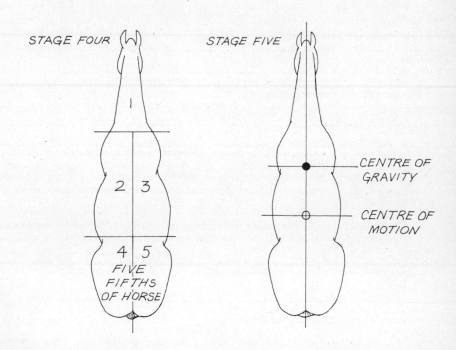

STAGE FOUR

1

2 | 3

4 | 5

FIVE
FIFTHS
OF HORSE

STAGE FIVE

CENTRE OF
GRAVITY

CENTRE OF
MOTION

Improving communications with the horse

Straight Lines

Using straight lines in the arena/school—i.e. correct work on straight lines—is very important and should be carried out with care, as this develops the straightening of the horse by reducing the lateral arcs along the horse's back, i.e., the length of the spine, without allowing the neck immediately in front of the withers—and the centre of the back—to become dipped or hollow.

● Correct straight line work carried out intelligently develops subtle lateral muscle co-ordination, improving the walk and canter gaits, by freeing the shoulder and hip joints of the fore and hind limbs on both sides of the horse. This in turn helps to reduce the tendency to 'dish' and/or 'plait' throughout the full length of the fore limbs.

● Correct straight line work encourages the lengthening/stretching of diagonal muscle co-ordination, and reduces the tendency to run at the trot, i.e., short, quick 'unprogressive' trot steps. It also tends to eliminate the 'rock and roll' which often interferes with the gaits, by encouraging whole limb stretch.

● Correct straight line work carried out effectively allows the rider to fully unite the horse with the minimum of physical effort, and to stabilise the correct convex/round outline, however faulty the conformation might be.

● Correct straight line work stabilises the horse's centre of gravity, and the centre of motion, improving the vertical balance (and movement) of the horse. It also prevents the normal tilting, and/or leaning inwards and/or outwards which develops stiff limb movement, so common with many riding horses.

● Correct straight line work on a light, long, or loose rein is the rider's best test for the *application of his own skills* when moving forward.

'. . . To master classical equitation it is essential to understand correct equine and human locomotion . . .'

'. . . The first component to decide the programme of the lesson is the quality—or lack of it—in a single gait, or one gait with another . . .'

'. . . Whenever you are schooling and training horses keep your mind full of equestrian thoughts . . .'

'. . . Where there is a healthy horse, there is strength, speed, and beauty . . .'

'. . . In good riding, the body above the waist should always be elegant, below the waist, i.e., the seat—should remain in contact with the saddle and become part of the horse in movement . . .'

'. . . There are times when the horse should be encouraged to go forward in self-carriage on a long and/or loose rein—this will show the rider whether his schooling and riding is correct . . .'

'. . . The upright horse, i.e., without tilting or leaning to one side or the other, has greater control of his balance, and develops much more suppleness in his limbs . . .'

'. . . Stirrup irons can be used as an aid to stabilise the body posture according to the task in hand, they are not intended to be used as permanent weight carriers for normal riding, i.e., for standing in and disturbing the seat . . .'

'. . . Lesson programmes lose their point if they are wholly "drill rides", without ever changing the position of the ride to encourage individual effort, responsibility, and gait control . . .'

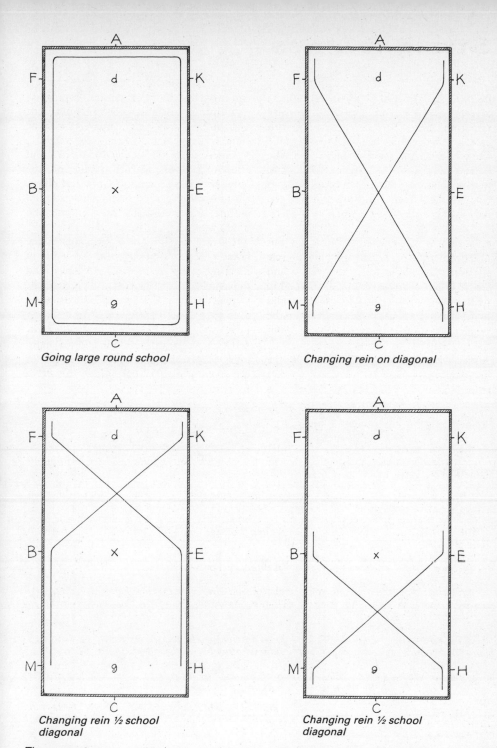

Going large round school

Changing rein on diagonal

Changing rein ½ school diagonal

Changing rein ½ school diagonal

The curves/arcs connecting one straight line with another depends on the standard of training of the horse, with minimum curve/arc being a part of a 6 metre diameter circle. Note that with many figures shown on this and the following pages, the rider can change rein as required.

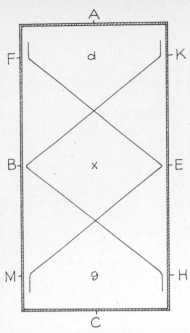

*Two ½ school diagonals
staying on same rein*

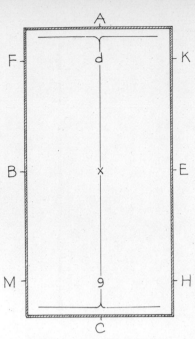

*Down centre/long ½ school
with/without change of rein*

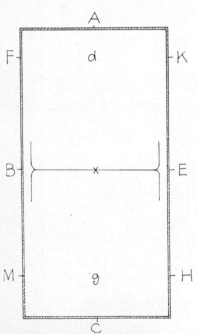

*Short ½ school with/without
change of rein*

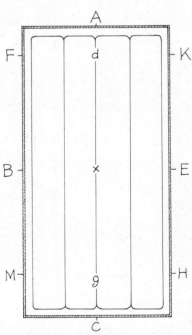

*Long ¾ school/long ½
school/long ¼ school—with/
without change of rein*

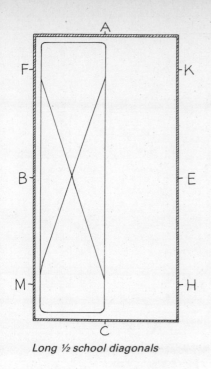

Long ½ school diagonals

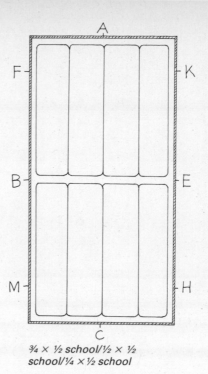

¾ × ½ school/½ × ½ school/¼ × ½ school

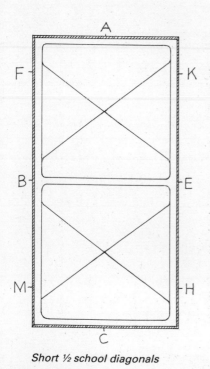

Short ½ school diagonals

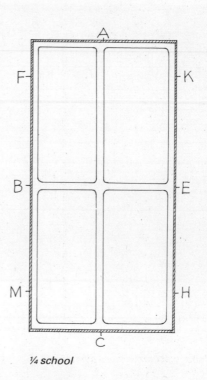

¼ school

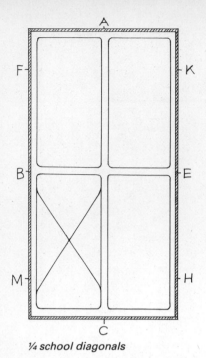

¼ school diagonals

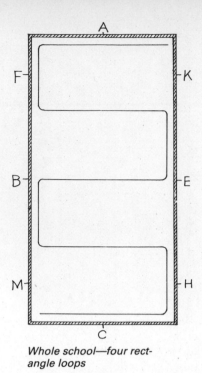

Whole school—four rect-angle loops

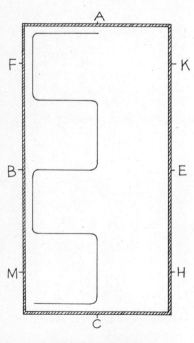

Long ½ school—four square loops

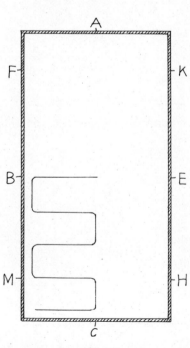

¼ school—four rectangle loops

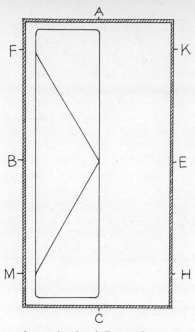

Long ½ school diagonals

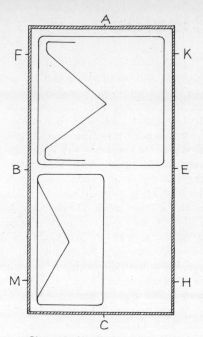

Short ½ school diagonals. ¼ school diagonals

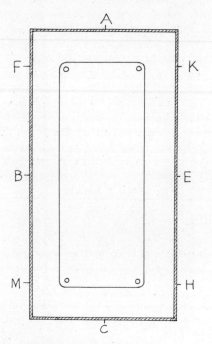

Working away from wall/ sides

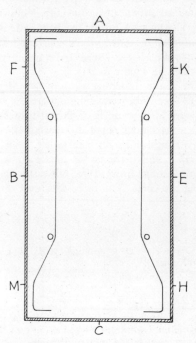

From wall to wall—straight lines

Circles

Using circles in the arena/school, or circling, is an ideal exercise for bringing horse and rider into harmony with the minimum of rider problems and the maximum of advantages, much easier than correct straight line work. On the circle the rider can be taught to use both reins correctly and independently—at one and the same time—while finding it relatively easy to maintain free forward movement. Do not try to hold the horse on the circle—which is physically impossible, anyway—by hanging onto the inside rein, and easing the outside rein. The whole horse must be ridden in a 'united' form, tracking correctly, in a pleasant even rhythm, and regular tempo, rather than pulling one quarter of the horse round on a circle, and abandoning the other three-quarters of the horse by loosening the outside rein.

The more controlled animation produced, the more the rider must keep the whole horse 'united' to carry out true and correct circles. The rider must sit upright, without stiffness, monitoring the energy, the gait, and the balance of the horse. On all circles and curves the rider sits square to axis.

The gentle stretching down of the rider's inside leg, while remaining square to axis prevents his posture from being disturbed while overcoming possible opposing effects of centrifugal and centripetal forces. That is, the rider, and/or the horse, sliding, tilting, and/or leaning inward or outward while riding the circle. The more advanced rider maintains the correct posture by varying the bracing of the back.

The rider's outside rein holds the horse to the size of the circle, as well as maintaining the true tracking of the four feet. The inside rein has two tasks, to gently and smoothly flex the horse's lower jaw—encouraging him to lightly 'chew' which encourages the flow of saliva, and according to his suppleness and balance, gently and 'feelingly' inviting him to flex his head and neck, so that the whole horse can follow the arc/circumference of the circle. The inside rein used incorrectly throws the horse's hind quarters outwards and away from the track, interfering with correct locomotion, and at the same time placing the horse at an angle to the direction of movement.

The hands play a critical part in the riding of circles, keeping the steering organised, preventing the horse's head tilting, keeping his inner shoulder light, and the lower jaw supple, preventing the horse moving sideward, and/or leaning inward/outward, while the rider's seat, and legs give support, keeping the equine power running smoothly.

Circles can be carried out singly, in any multiple, or follow one with another when moving round the track. Full circles and half-circles can be joined to make up figure-of-eights, or half figure-of-eights. The following circle diagrams should inspire the rider to develop programmes as an aid to improved riding. Remember it is quality not quantity of circle riding which is important.

'. . . If you can ride at each gait with rein contacts between 20 and 100 grammes—you have a light hand . . .'

Note   A circle is a continuous line at a constant radius to one point. In National and International dressage the following two definitions are used:
1 A circle—is over 6 metres diameter
2 A volte—is a circle of 6 metres diameter
In the circle diagrams shown opposite and on the following pages the abbreviation 'm/d'= metres diameter. All circle dimensions shown are approximate.

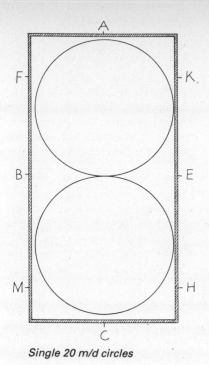

Single 20 m/d circles

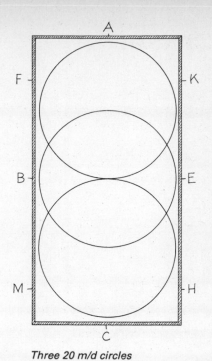

Three 20 m/d circles

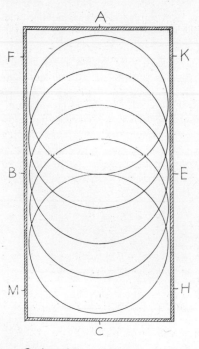

Series of 20 m/d circles

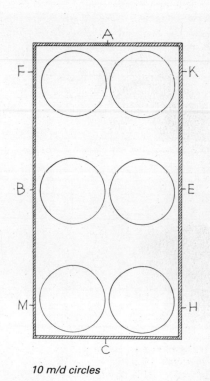

10 m/d circles

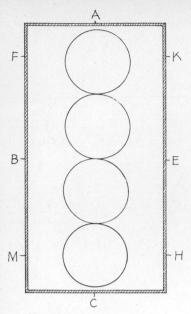

10 m/d circles on a centre line

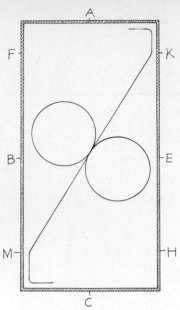

10 m/d circles on diagonal

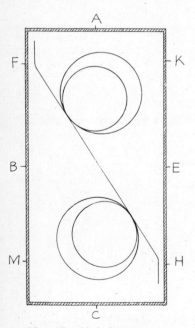

10 to 15 m/d circles on diagonal

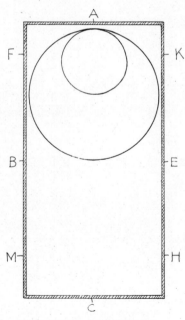

10 m/d circle from 20 m/d circle

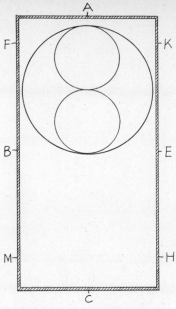

Two×10 m/d circles from 20
m/d circle

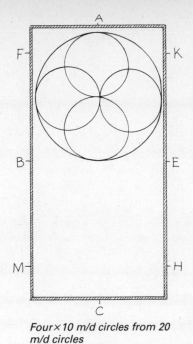

Four×10 m/d circles from 20
m/d circles

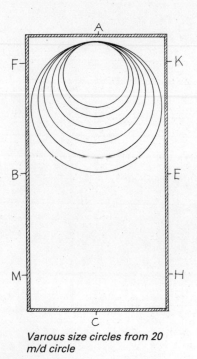

Various size circles from 20
m/d circle

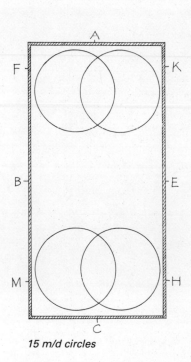

15 m/d circles

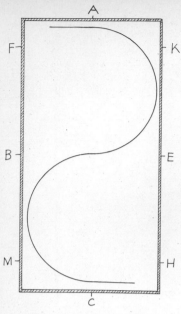

½ figure-of-eight using 20 m/d circles

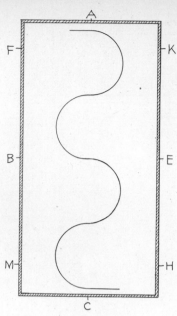

10 m/d ½ circle serpentine

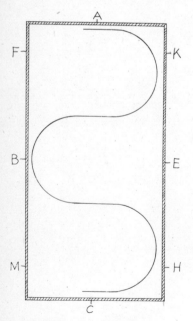

Three loop serpentine— whole arena

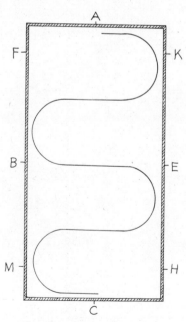

Four loop serpentine— whole arena

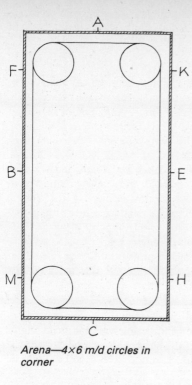

Arena—4×6 m/d circles in
corner

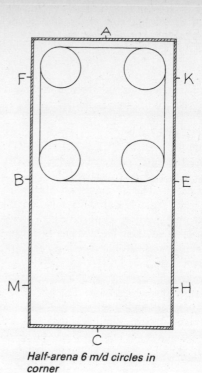

Half-arena 6 m/d circles in
corner

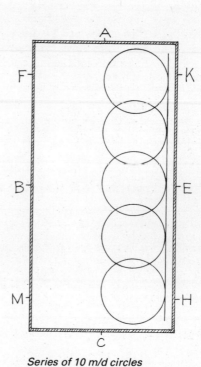

Quarter-arena 5 m/d circles
in corner

Series of 10 m/d circles

Turns

There are four normal ways of turning a horse right or left when mounted.

Quarter of a circle

Where the horse's hind legs follow the track of the forelegs, and can be carried out in walk, trot, canter, and gallop.

Advantages The advantages are numerous. The rider's hands introduce and lead the horse into the curve, while the legs and body assist in maintaining forward movement and balance according to the speed and gait, and the size of the curve/turn.

Turns on the fore hand

To be carried out at walk only.

Advantages Has limited advantages in general equitation and dressage riding. Is invaluable as an exercise for outdoor riding as an aid when opening and closing gates. Activates the hind quarters, hip joints and hind limbs.

Hands resist but do not pull backward while the legs act to move the hind quarters to the side. The hind limbs move sidewards while the horse turns/pivots/marking time with the inner fore limb.

Turn on the centre

To be carried out at the walk only.

Advantages Has limited advantages in general equitation. Permits the rider to learn and develop the co-ordination of hand and leg aids to direct the movement of the horse around his centre. Activates the joints of all four limbs.

Hands and legs act simultaneously with the fore and hind limbs moving round a pivot area between the position of the horse's centre of gravity, and his centre of motion.

Turns on the haunches

Known also as pirouettes. Can be carried out at walk, piaffe (extreme collected trot), and the canter.

Advantages Numerous advantages in the practical applications of horsemanship. Activates and strengthens the main motor forces of the horse. Supples and lightens the forehand. Aids in collecting and uniting the horse.

Hands lead and guide the forehand sidewards—never backward—The rider's legs maintain and support the hands in providing the correct amount of impulsion. Initially the horse is taught to move forward/sideward at one and the same time, retaining his true gait while the hind limbs traverse a small circle, which is reduced in size until the inner hind limb acts as a 'stepping' pivot.

'... It is only possible to plant in the horse's mind, that which is in the character of his rider ...'

'... When the rider feels he can carry out and ride smooth transitions, the time is ripe for further study, and learning the many correct stages of using the braced back ...'

'... If the horse is nervous—the rider instils confidence by natural and/or developed equestrian tact, combined with equestrian skills ...'

'... When riding, the function of equine muscle is to work, the function of human muscle is to guide, encourage and permit ...'

'... The main quality of a good rider is to improve a difficult horse, the main quality of the good horse is to improve the indifferent rider ...'

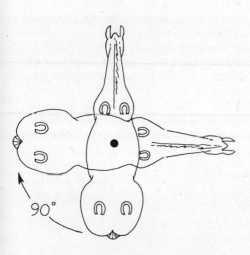

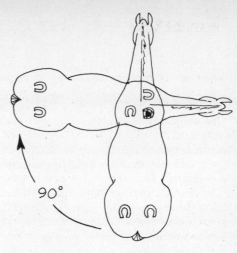

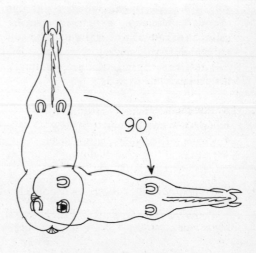

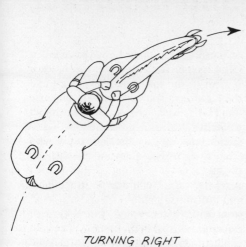

TURNING RIGHT
ON A QUARTER
OF A CIRCLE

TURNING RIGHT
ON THE FOREHAND

TURNING RIGHT
ON THE CENTRE

TURNING RIGHT ON
THE HAUNCHES OR HINDQUARTERS
(1/4 PIROUETTE)

Four methods of turning

Gaits—Correct and Incorrect

Riding within a normal range of speeds should help the rider to develop the correct mode of locomotion, by fully utilising the musculature of the horse. The gait speeds are:

- Walk—4-time   3 to 5 mph approximately (5 to 8 kph)
- Trot—2-time   3 to 10 mph approximately (5 to 16 kph)
- Canter—3-time   3 to 15 mph approximately (5 to 24 kph)
- Gallop—4-time   6 to 25 mph approximately (10 to 40 kph)

Obviously, the rider must follow a sensible gait proportion, i.e., one gait to another, during the work, exercise, and schooling of the horse to avoid producing faulty locomotion, evasions and resistances when the horse is in movement. Faulty locomotion is built-up and developed—even by so-called experts who over-develop specific muscles, or groups of specific muscles, in one or more particular gaits, often resulting in damaging effects to the horse's way of moving.

A reasonable average gait proportion per hour for a fit horse can be listed as:

- Walk—20 minutes approximately
- Trot—30 minutes approximately
- Canter—10 minutes approximately
- Gallop—3 minutes/reducing trot to approximately 27 minutes

Faults to avoid are:

- Walk—Too slow with minimum activity —dragging of any feet—running with two, three, or four feet.
- Trot—Too slow causing the dragging of the hind feet, and in extremely bad cases, fore feet as well. Too fast and 'running' in diagonals, i.e., short, quick steps with stiff or slack limbs not embracing any forward freedom and swing from the shoulders and thighs.
- Canter—Too tight and/or stiff, running and difficult to hold, i.e., running—trot in front with canter behind, trot behind with canter in front, or both, running trot in front and behind with the impression of a three or four beat lollop.
- Gallop—Too heavy and lying 'hard' on the hands—reducing the efficiency of the drive/power from the hind quarters and hind limbs.

Dressage variants within each gait:

- Collected—Active, elevated, and fully controlled shortened steps developing increased limb flexion
- Working—Pleasant energetic gait. Fully utilising the horse's musculature in a way which improves the horse's general fitness and balance
- Medium—Horse moving parallel to the ground with longer—but not quicker—steps/strides, with the average horse over-tracking one to two hoof prints.
- Extended—Moving parallel to the ground with longer—not quicker—steps/strides, with the average horse overtracking approximately 3 to 4 hoof prints.

'... If a horse is not 'united'—physically and mentally—it is impossible to have a good ride. If a horse is not correctly 'collected', the rider will never be able to carry out advanced equestrian airs with ease, grace and lightness ...'

'... Horse and rider each have a brain and a body—when in harmony complete orchestration will result ...'

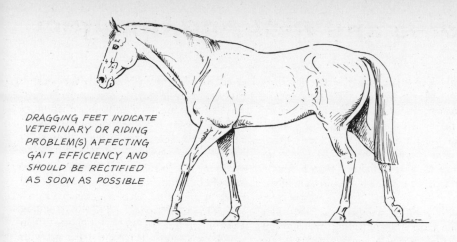

DRAGGING FEET INDICATE
VETERINARY OR RIDING
PROBLEM(S) AFFECTING
GAIT EFFICIENCY AND
SHOULD BE RECTIFIED
AS SOON AS POSSIBLE

~ *INCORRECT* HINGES FROM THE TOE ~

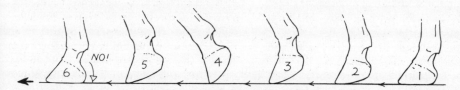

INCORRECT - DRAGGING FEET HORSE'S TOES NEVER LEAVE THE GROUND.
IN SOFT GOING THEY SINK AND 'GROOVE' THE GROUND. AT THE END OF STEP
THE FOOT IS RETARDED AS THE HEEL COMES DOWN LAST ROLLING BACKWARDS

~ *CORRECT* HINGES FROM THE HEEL ~

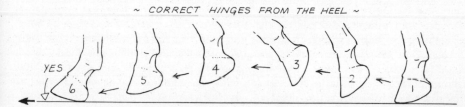

CORRECT LOCOMOTION COMMENCING EACH STEP THE HEEL LEAVES THE
GROUND FIRST. AT THE END OF EACH STEP THE HEEL COMES TO THE GROUND
FIRST ENSURING PROGRESSIVE LOCOMOTION

Equine locomotion, showing some intermittent phases of a single step

---

Note Excessive amounts of correct walk—the emphasis being on the term correct—does not
in any way interfere with the other three gaits. But any slowly increasing amount of incorrect
walk/trot/canter and gallop will eventually affect the overall efficiency of all the gaits.

77

Horse and Rider Jumping

The rider's position when jumping obstacles up to 3 feet 6 inches (110 centimetres, approximately) and with a similar spread, from flat level ground, is caught extremely well in the illustration. The rider's head, neck, and spine are the critical factors in ensuring the rider's balance is in harmony with the balance of the horse throughout the jump.

The illustration shows horse and rider jumping at an efficient 'canter' speed over a spread fence/obstacle—not too fast and not too slow—with a normal/natural tension holding the head, neck, and spine of horse and rider in a sound mechanical outline. The rider is giving the horse—and himself—the best possible chance of clearing the (imaginary) obstacle, without any unnecessary physical interference.

Any rounding of the rider's back (spine), makes it extremely difficult for the rider to carry his head and neck correctly, which in turn reduces the rider's efficiency and balance causing a tendency to 'rock 'n' roll' forward/backward, and sometimes even sideward, as the horse modifies his outline/posture in the approach, take-off, jump, landing, and getting away.

All successful jumping depends on the rider creating the ideal conditions in speed and balance on the flat approaching the obstacle(s) so that the horse has the maximum chance of clearing the obstacle(s) with the minimum disturbance and interfer-ence from the rider—permitting the horse to take the obstacle with the minimum of effort, physical and mental.

Where there is a safety factor concerned, i.e., jumping at racing speeds where the take-off and landing over each obstacle can be different on account of the undulating terrain, or interference by another horse and rider by bumping, or being crowded into a fence, the sensible rider adopts 'a safety first' position in the saddle. This ensures that whatever happens, the rider has the best possible chance of survival—staying in the saddle—and in a position of control and balance to proceed to the next obstacle. This safety first posture is one where the rider's body remains vertical—or slightly behind the vertical—according to the type of obstacle, wide spreads, drop fences, etc., so that if the horse 'pecks' or stumbles on landing, the rider is in a better position to avoid being catapulted over the horse's head. This safety first posture can be seen and studied with interest in the photographs which appear in the equestrian and national press during the steeplechasing season, especially those seen on television of the Grand National. *All seats and postures when jumping have their relevant importance when applied to the task on hand*, and the wise rider is the one who can jump any obstacle and give his horse and himself the greatest chance of being able to continue with the minimum of delay and effort to both.

'. . . Correctly controlled movement of the horse's head and neck—combined with the correct use of the rider's body—ensures equine equilibrium and efficiency . . .'

'. . . When riding, if a movement or experience feels beautiful, it is correct . . .'

'. . . The faster the gait, the quicker the rider must think and act . . .'

'. . . Lead in with the correct exercises, and the most advanced figures/movements become relatively easy . . .'

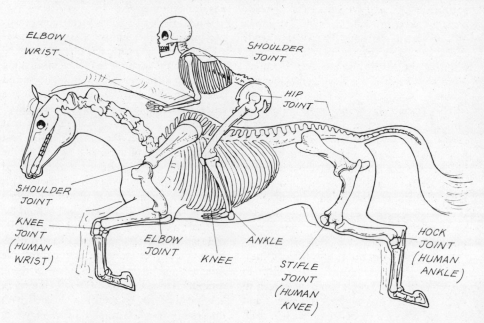

ELBOW
WRIST
SHOULDER JOINT
HIP JOINT
SHOULDER JOINT
KNEE JOINT (HUMAN WRIST)
ELBOW JOINT
KNEE
ANKLE
STIFLE JOINT (HUMAN KNEE)
HOCK JOINT (HUMAN ANKLE)

Comparative skeletons of horse and rider in action

The Riding Teacher/Instructor

Some Technical Considerations

'. . . Good riding teachers must keep quenching their everlasting thirst for equestrian scholarship . . .'

Grading of Riders

One of the greatest difficulties in riding schools and riding establishments is the accurate grading of riders so that they can be sensibly put with others of a similar standard. Otherwise it is known that many riders/students/and pupils, often feel that they have been 'miscast', and placed with those not as good, or much too skilful, so that they immediately have doubts about carrying on with further lessons/rides.

This often leads to very keen riding enthusiasts—whatever their standard—visiting as many schools as possible in search for the correct one. The following suggestions are made so that the teacher/instructor, can ask the rider at what particular grade, he or she considers they are capable of riding. This will save time, embarrassment, possibly expensive accidents necessitating litigation, as well as putting the pupil/rider at ease with the staff, who can then allot the pupil/rider a suitable horse, or pony.

Beginner rider

A rider who knows very little indeed about horses and ponies, and needs to be under continual supervision in an enclosed school, or arena.

Novice rider

A rider who can manage a quiet, obedient horse or pony, in an enclosed school, or arena under supervision. Is able to go out for a hack, or ride if properly escorted by a responsible person(s). Can walk, trot, and canter an obedient horse, or pony, and jump small obstacles up to approximately 18 inches (45 centimetres), all riding activities being carried out under supervision.

Average rider

A rider able to saddle-up, mount, and take an obedient horse, or pony into the school, arena, or out on exercise with another competent rider. Can handle the horse, or pony in all gaits and transitions with confidence, always maintaining full control. Able to jump various small obstacles up to approximately 30 inches (75 centimetres) in height and spread. Will always return the horse to the stable, dry and comfortable, and is able to remove all the tack, and rug-up.

Advanced rider

A rider capable of competing in small local shows, novice and preliminary dressage tests, small show jumping competitions, and a one day event. Knows how to attend to their horse's or pony's welfare, in all branches of horsemastership, grooming, bandaging, first aid, cleaning and fitting of saddlery, feeding and watering, etc. Capable of acting as an escort with assistance, and possibly holding some recognised qualifications.

Being aware of the number of accidents—some fatal—which seem to be increasing in number each year, and involve litigation, sometimes going on for years, it would appear that some knowledge of the rider/pupil's equestrian capability might have prevented many serious riding accidents. Under no circumstances whatsoever should any rider(s) be allowed to leave a riding establishment mounted, unless those responsible have seen the rider(s) handle their horses at walk/trot and canter, to their fullest satisfaction—and for the first ride out, a competent escort should attend to assess the rider's ability.

'... For a new sensation when riding collected gaits, try picking the horse up with your thighs and a correctly braced back, while at the same time elevating your body upward/forward, all at one and the same time ...'

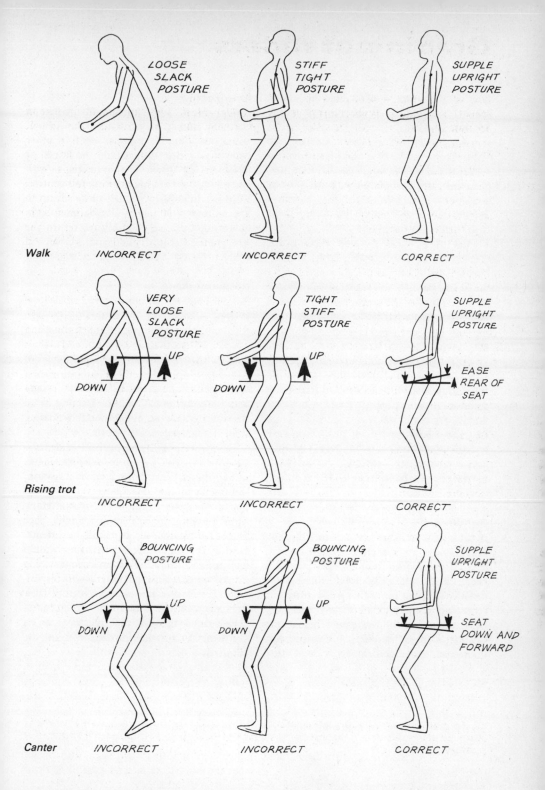

Walk

LOOSE SLACK POSTURE — INCORRECT

STIFF TIGHT POSTURE — INCORRECT

SUPPLE UPRIGHT POSTURE — CORRECT

Rising trot

VERY LOOSE SLACK POSTURE — UP DOWN — INCORRECT

TIGHT STIFF POSTURE — UP DOWN — INCORRECT

SUPPLE UPRIGHT POSTURE — EASE REAR OF SEAT — CORRECT

Canter

BOUNCING POSTURE — UP DOWN — INCORRECT

BOUNCING POSTURE — UP DOWN — INCORRECT

SUPPLE UPRIGHT POSTURE — SEAT DOWN AND FORWARD — CORRECT

83

Rider Considerations

1. The primary concern of the riding teacher/instructor at all times is the safety of the rider/pupil.

2. The pupil/rider—unless known and experienced—must never be left unattended or outside of the range/vision of the teacher.

3. The teacher/instructor must always explain the requirements in the most simple terms and without using equestrian jargon.

4. Reasonable time must always be allowed for the pupil/rider to assimilate the request, requirements, and instructions of the teacher/instructor.

5. The teacher/instructor must always clearly describe what is required—and if necessary demonstrate the requirement, in the area the pupil has to carry out the work, and which lends itself to effective and efficient execution.

6. The teacher/instructor must never allow horse and rider to take up a posture, and/or position, which can disturb and/or interfere with the required result.

7. The teacher/instructor must be experienced enough to 'feel' what horse and rider are carrying out, so that evasions and resistances can be minimised at the earliest possible moment.

8. The teacher/instructor must be fully conversant with the mechanics of all exercises, figures, and gaits which they are trying to pass on to the pupil/rider.

9. The teacher/instructor should occasionally ride the pupil's horse—at least once a month—whether the horse is used for private lessons, or used in school rides—so that they have a practical assessment of the horse's qualities, and/or limitations. This prevents unreasonable demands being made of horse and rider.

10. No pupil will ever make much progress without the maximum of practical work/riding which can be fitted into each lesson, so keep the theory to a working minimum, and avoid lectures when in the school or arena.

11. Theoretical lessons when dismounted can be valuable.

12. Never create serious mental blocks, or fears about various movements, exercises, figures, gaits, and gait variants. Classical horsemanship is within the scope of every rider, providing the teacher/instructor is an expert, and fully understands what, why, and how they are teaching horse and rider.

13. The teacher/instructor's primary aim must be to make every moment of every lesson, interesting, educational, absorbing, and fun.

14. The teaching of correct posture is critical if the rider is to be given an established foundation upon which all progress depends, i.e.,

• Upright body posture, not in front of the vertical.

• Use of the legs—together and independently—without altering the body posture.

• Use of the hands, i.e., the correct handling of the reins, without body movement, and with minimal arm movement/swinging.

• To learn how to use the braced-back as part of the mechanism—with the seat—of absorbing the movement of the horse.

15. Moving at fast speeds disturbs the initial postural qualities of the rider. When the rider can hold a reasonably good basic posture—then, and then only—attempt speed variants.

16. The number of bad and/or difficult days in the year with any one pupil/rider, irrespective of his/her standard, should never exceed those which can be counted on one hand. If they do, there is something radically wrong somewhere, which calls for a careful analysis from the teacher/instructor, even to the point of the teacher/instructor having to admit that they have possibly reached the limit of their practical scholarship. If this is found to be the reason, with amicable agreement, the pupil and possibly the teacher/instructor should seek further—and more advanced—instruction.

17. The mystical union between horse and rider is felt, rather than seen, and by its inexplicable nature is somewhat difficult to impart in theory alone.

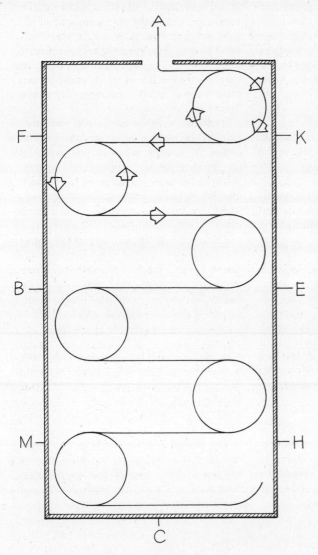

When first entering the riding school/arena some horses become a little difficult and naughty, occasionally causing falls and accidents. Once the riders have mounted and adjusted the stirrups and tightened the girth, they should immediately occupy the horse mentally and physically at the walk, by carrying out some simple—but correct—figure riding. Never aimlessly wander about, usually going large, with long/loose reins until you have satisfied yourself that the horse is reasonably calm. The illustration on this page is simply a 'suggestion', but there are literally hundreds of variants of figure combinations which the ordinary rider can carry out to settle their horses— and to improve their riding skills—at an active walk

Mentally alert horse and rider

Arena/School/Manege

Riding tuition should always be given in a correctly proportioned, sized, enclosed arena—covered or otherwise—in an environment which lends itself to a direct communication between teacher/instructor, horse and rider. Counter attractions should be kept to a minimum until the rider is capable of handling the horse with confidence at walk, trot and canter.

Surface

The surface of the arena/school/manege, both indoors and outdoors, should give the horse a good footing.

Indoors The surface should not be too soft, too deep, too dry, nor too dusty. A balanced mixture of bark, sand and granulated plastic should be ideal for individual and class work.

Outdoors The surface must be well laid on a good draining base, where there is a slight slope on the land, running from one long side down to the opposite long side. A correct type of modified membrane to aid quick draining, and a balanced mixture of hard bark, sand, and granulated plastic, laid to a good workable depth, not too deep, or too shallow, has proved to be workable all the year round.

With all floors and surfaces, a little daily care in keeping it raked and level improves its efficiency and working life. Wherever possible white paint/distemper should be used to 'outline' outdoor maneges, and on the lower walls/boards of riding schools.

Markers, Cones, or 'Bloks'

It is useful to have at least twelve plastic cones as markers, similar to those used by public authorities for traffic diversion, and public work on roadways. Also, where possible, a set of letters, permanently fixed, identical to those used in dressage tests and correctly spaced, will be found to be an additional valuable aid when teaching directional figures and movements.

'Bloks' are a registered product, and can be used in the same way as the cones, but of course the main advantage is their suitability for building jumps, quickly and simply. Without having to drag around, uprights, metal cups, and loose metal pins, wings, etc., which can be dangerous and involve much labour.

The cones and 'Bloks' have their value in assisting horse and rider to carry out accurate figures, e.g., circles of differing sizes, without distracting horse and rider. This assists the rider to concentrate on improving his riding and the horse, rather than have to get too deeply involved in the shape of the circle.

When the riding of circles around markers becomes second nature—the rider will find that subconsciously he is able to ride accurately shaped circles, instead of awkward shapes which are supposed to be 'circles'.

The dressage letters correctly positioned and fixed, familiarise the rider with dressage test figures and movements, when changing direction, or modifying the gaits, i.e., transitions, including gait variants.

'. . . Equestrian ability is most easily recognisable in the simplest of movements . . .'

'. . . Equestrian science is for the student—equestrian art for the expert . . .'

'. . . In horsemanship there are correct and incorrect ways of doing everything, the correct way pays dividends, and the incorrect way always results in more work and trouble . . .'

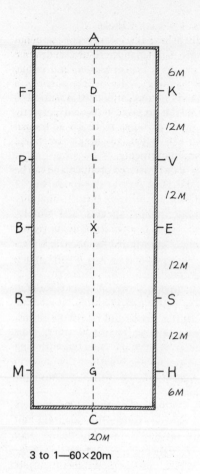

3 to 1—60×20m

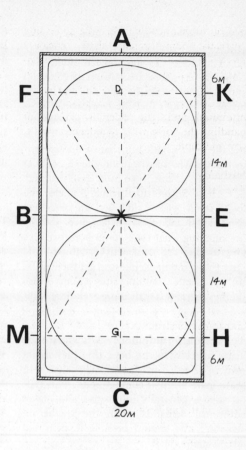

2 to 1—40×20m

Arena sizes should be based on the smallest workable unit 20×20 metre square. Then, in the following sizes: two to one—40×20 metres; three to one—60×20 metres. With available space there is no reason why the smallest unit should not be a 30 metre square—ideal for working young horses. But the multiples should still be two and three to one

20M x 20M

1 to 1—20m square

The Riding Lesson

Riding lessons usually fall into four main groups:

1. Those for genuine novice riders and complete beginners, which start off exciting, and after a few weeks become dull and boring because the rider feels he has learnt it all—and for some unknown reason is not allowed to go galloping across open country. This is not the rider's fault but that of the teacher/instructor who has been unable to conduct those early lessons in an intelligent manner.

2. Those lessons for ordinary riders who look upon each ride as an excellent educational and social experience, usually not minding what they do on horseback, so long as they are kept actively amused and interested, and in each lesson get their walk, trot, and canter, with possibly a jump or two thereby learning a little more each time. This gradual progress is rewarding to both pupil and teacher/instructor.

3. Lessons for ambitious riders who wish to learn correctly in the hope that they might own a horse or pony themselves, or participate in small competitions. This type of rider is generally inquisitive and makes additional demands upon the teacher/instructor, who should be able to help and advise such riders.

4. Finally, there is a group of riders—larger than imagined—whose ambition is to take up 'horses' professionally. In many cases they hope that with hard work and study they might well become qualified riding teachers/instructors. Of the four groups, it is the first and the last which make the greatest demands on the teacher/instructor, both requiring extra special care and attention, with all pupils/riders enjoying their lessons.

I have not forgotten the disabled riders, but they have their own organisation, run by a wonderful band of hard working volunteers from many professional categories.

A good riding teacher/instructor must put life, inspiration, interest, and a little scholarship into the riding lesson, otherwise they will fall short of the qualities the intelligent pupil expects. Lessons do not consist of a continuous monotonous mechanical drone of 'parrot instruction'. Good practice, sensible analysis and discussion after the lesson is the key to success.

Ingredients for sensible lessons

- The lesson must be stimulating, enjoyable, and an educational experience . . .
- Must be based upon correct gait applications, sequence/proportion/quantity . . .
- Should include correct figure/movement sequences—not too demanding . . .
- Based upon horse and rider's physical—and mental—fitness . . .
- Lessons should be modified to suit temperature/climatic conditions . . .
- The rider should be corrected—but never disillusioned . . .
- There should always be respect and good manners between teacher/horse/pupil . . .
- Good lessons eliminate faults—not manufacture them . . .
- Intelligent lessons establish a good rapport between teacher/horse/pupil . . .
- Encourage confidence under good conditions with long and loose rein riding . . .
- Do not carry out excessive amounts of work which produce loose/slack horses/riders.
- Avoid practical jokes—an element of danger always exists in riding . . .
- Finally—it is the *quality*—not the *quantity*—which gives each lesson its value.

Note Gaits to be mastered in order of merit:–
Group 1—Walk, sitting trot, and rising trot.
Group 2—Walk, sitting trot, rising trot, and canter.
Groups 3 & 4—Walk, sitting trot, rising trot, canter, and gallop.

. . . Mickey was an Irishman with a great way with a horse. They came to hand and prospered under his guidance. In the terms of fifty years ago he was a great nagsman. At schooling horses he was a fine schoolmaster. They went well for him and were always beautifully balanced. Active they were and graceful, but never "busy". Nor fussy, neither he nor his horse. "What is your system, Mickey?" said an owner. "How do you set about your schooling? How do you know what to do next?" "Sure, your honour", says Mickey, "the horse tells me." Let that be the motto for the trainer, the teacher, the instructor.

In the horse world we need instructors. Not amiable parrots. They must observe, assess, analyse, conclude, impart—and inspire. Much learning comes from imitation: an instructor needs to be a good enough horseman to be copiable. But better a poorish horseman who can teach, than a good horseman who teaches poorly. And what use to a proprietor or chief instructor of an establishment is an assistant who does not improve every horse ridden? . . .

(Brigadier J. C. Friedberger, DSO, DL)

Figure Riding

All figures carried out in the riding school or arena, are made up of straight lines of varying lengths, and circles—or parts of circles—down to a minimum of 6 metres diameter.

Where the horse is moving forward and sideward at one and the same time—lateral work—these figures can also be carried out on straight lines and circles, with the horse moving on two, three, or four tracks. When carrying out lateral work, the horse is either looking in the direction of movement, or, away from the direction of movement. The angles of lateral work commence at approximately 5 degrees and can be carried out up to a maximum of approximately 30 degrees. Lateral work requires a supple and well-balanced horse.

A good teacher introduces—and I emphasise the word 'introduces'—the rider to these various figures in their less demanding form, during their first thirty to forty lessons. In this way the pupil/rider does not look upon certain figures and exercises as something mysterious, and far beyond their ability. There is no reason whatsoever, on the correct horse and with a good teacher, why an absolute beginner should not be given the feel of a turn on the haunches, or lateral work at the walk.

Good teachers/instructors should always try to avoid giving all riders—beginners and advanced—mental blocks, i.e., a sub-conscious fear of attempting to carry out some of the more interesting figures, exercises, and movements in equitation. It is much wiser, and more helpful to the rider to encourage him to attempt these more exciting aspects of horsemanship, perhaps for only one or two correct steps at walk, than to repetitively suggest it will be at least twelve months or more before they will ever be able to attempt such 'advanced' work.

The intelligent teaching of figure riding at the walk is an excellent way to teach and prepare the beginner and novice rider in the correct use of their natural aids, i.e., correct use of body posture, correct use of the legs, and correct use of the hands. In fact with advanced riders who have developed bad postural faults, it is only at the walk where they can be analysed and permanently corrected. This type of approach helps to keep riders mentally and physically alert, keeps the horse interested, and prevents the teacher becoming—or appearing—bored.

The riding teacher/instructor must try to be more inventive, and develop a little ingenuity in connection with the mental occupation of the pupil/rider, and horse. Composing new figures, or possibly using some of the older classical school figures, e.g., the square—of 20, 15, and 10 metres—to encourage and develop active, and correct, gaits when carrying out quarter pirouettes at walk, and canter. It is of great value to all concerned for the teacher to sow seeds of equestrian originality, with new equestrian interpretation.

'. . . The main aid for gait elevation is the correct bracing of the rider's back—not the action of the hand . . .'

'. . . Aimlessly going large around the manege is a sure way of confirming evasions and resistances . . .'

'. . . Some horses are born brilliant—and are few and far between—the majority of horses need reasonable care and attention to become good rides in the riding school, and outdoors . . .'

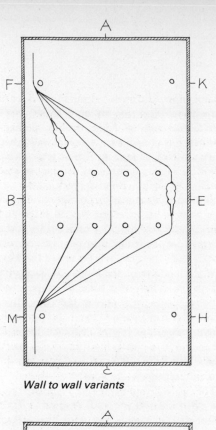

Wall to wall variants

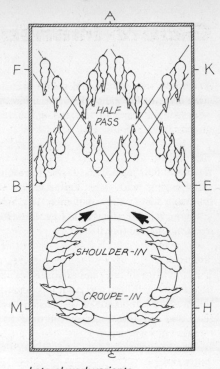

Lateral work variants

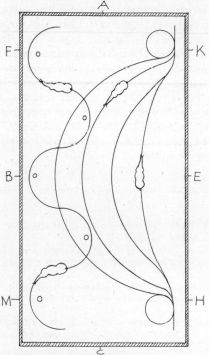

Circle/curve variants

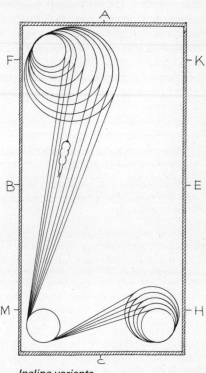

Incline variants

Innovative figure riding

Gait Variants

The walk, trot, canter and gallop are each clear and distinct gaits which the interested rider should learn to feel, recognise, and understand.

The walk
Is 4-time; four separate beats on the ground, commencing with any limb/foot in the following consecutive sequence, left hind, left fore, right hind, and right fore. Hind foot overtracking the fore foot.

The trot
Is 2-time; two distinct and separate beats on the ground, left hind and right fore together followed by a moment of suspension, right hind and left fore together followed by a moment of suspension.

The canter
Is 3-time; single hind limb, diagonal pair of limbs together, single fore limb, followed by a moment of suspension. Left hind, right hind and left fore together, right fore followed by a moment of suspension . . .
or,
Right hind, left hind and right fore together, left fore followed by a moment of suspension.

The gallop
(Transverse) Is 4-time; the two hind limbs/feet follow each other in quick succession, and in the same sequence the two fore limbs/feet follow each other in quick succession, followed by a moment of suspension. Right hind/left hind, right fore/left fore followed by a moment of suspension . . .
or,
Left hind/right hind, left fore/right fore, followed by a moment of suspension.

While it is important for the riding teacher/instructor to fully understand the detailed gait mechanics, the pupil/rider should be taught that at the various gaits, i.e., the four variants within each gait, *while maintaining the same rhythm* of correct equine locomotion in that particular gait, the horse is moving at four different speeds/tempos.

The walk, trot, canter and gallop, are described and defined here in their universally accepted 'elementary form', and not in the more 'advanced eight-phase stride'. Because the 'eight-phase stride' appears to be a totally unknown quantity to riding and dressage experts, their gait assessments leave much to be desired.

'. . . When involved with mounted equestrian problems—avoid weakening your own stability by flinging and/or opening your arms and permitting the horse to unite himself . . .'

'. . . Commonsense dictates that the speed of the ride should not exceed that of the slowest horse and rider, otherwise accidents result. "Match and position" your ride, so that no-one is placed in jeopardy . . .'

'. . . Never miss an opportunity to check your girth(s) to ensure they are correctly adjusted, and prevent the correctly fitted saddle from moving and/or twisting . . .'

'. . . Always ask for a "lead" (by another horse and rider) if you are having problems, sheer force seldom works and usually aggravates the situation . . .'

Note   There is no working walk in the FEI definitions. The fourth walk variant is described as 'Free walk'. Although in no way concise and conclusive, interested riding teachers/instructors and pupils will find much of interest in the FEI *Definitions of Gaits and Movements*.

APPROXIMATE GAIT VARIANTS - HIND FOOT SHADED/FOREFOOT NOT SHADED

HIND   *FORE*   *DIRECTION OF MOVEMENT*

COLLECTED GAIT

*UNDER-TRACKING APP. ONE OR TWO HOOFPRINTS
HIND FOOT UNDERTRACKS FORE FOOT*

*HIND
FORE*

WORKING GAIT

*TRACKING
HIND FOOT STEPS INTO
TRACK OF FORE FOOT*

FORE   *HIND*

MEDIUM GAIT

*OVER-TRACKING, APP. ONE TO TWO HOOFPRINTS
HIND FOOT OVERTRACKS THE TRACK OF
THE FORE FOOT*

FORE   *HIND*

EXTENDED GAIT

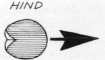

*OVER-TRACKING, APP. THREE TO FOUR HOOFPRINTS
HIND FOOT OVERSTEPS THE TRACK OF
THE FORE FOOT*

The illustrations on this page show variants, similar to F.E.I. (International Equestrian Federation) definitions of the gaits:

Collected gait—shortened/elevated/pleasantly activated steps/stride
Working gait—normal active gait for general schooling and exercise
Medium gait—lengthened and slightly more energetic steps/strides
Extended gait—maximum lengthening of united horse when stepping/striding

Left versus Right Handedness

Brain

The brain of the human being weighs around 1450 grammes, approximately one fiftieth of the total weight. The brain is divided into two parts which are almost symmetrical, the right side being mainly responsible for the control of the left side of the body, and the left side of the brain mainly responsible for the control of the right side of the body, both sides of the brain also having other separate functions.

Human body

Although the general appearance of the human body seen as a vertical posture from the front suggests that both sides—right and left halves—are identical, on closer examination it has been discovered that there are differences, e.g., that the right arm is often slightly longer than the left arm; that the left leg is slightly longer than the right leg; the better eye is usually the right eye. Also, there is some difference in the position of internal organs, more to one side than the other. All in all, it can be seen that on close investigation we are not perfectly symmetrical, which in many ways can have some bearing on our riding.

The horse—horizontal posture

It is a well known fact that most horses have a 'favoured' side, and this is usually to the left, i.e., the curvature to the left, which appears to bias the horse's centre of gravity slightly to the left. Over the years many theories have been put forward, e.g., the foetus lies curved to the left; when handled the foal is always approached from the left; the foal is always led from the left; the foal and all horses are always turned to the left, etc. Equine locomotion also throws up some very interesting facets which do not seem to have been investigated, i.e., the physical advantages and disadvantages of 'diagonal' versus 'lateral' modes of progression, probably the cause of many rider problems as well as gait irregularities.

Mental and physical development

It is impossible to lay down any hard and fast rules, because horses and riders vary so much in their temperaments, and what might well be applicable to one horse, or one rider, might not be to another. But it seems reasonable enough that putting a left-handed rider on a left-handed (sided) horse, and a right-handed rider on a right-handed (sided) horse is unlikely to produce a harmonious combination of balanced horse and rider.

There are numerous physical feelings, and mental attitudes and reactions which are very difficult to describe and impart in theory, and are best learnt, understood, and acquired from the back of the horse when riding. A great amount of correct practice is necessary to develop that splendid partnership, which makes itself apparent in the finished/polished horse and rider, who make even the simplest acts of horsemanship look elegant, graceful, and pure, i.e., classical equitation. A major achievement when the full facts of human anatomy and physiology are combined with equine anatomy and physiology, making horse and rider into true partners in the art of expressing joy through movement, by the co-ordination of different mental and physical qualities.

'. . . A bent and/or twisted buckle "hinged tongue" (pin) has caused many an accident, make sure all buckles and keepers are in good mechanical order, and are used correctly to secure reins, etc. . . .'

'. . . Sounds made with the voice are very important riding aids—talk to your horse—as a complement to the application of leg and hand . . .'

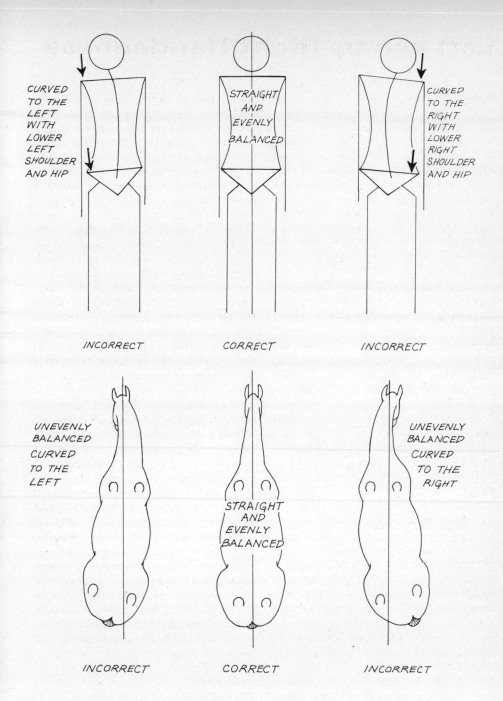

CURVED
TO THE
LEFT
WITH
LOWER
LEFT
SHOULDER
AND HIP

STRAIGHT
AND
EVENLY
BALANCED

CURVED
TO THE
RIGHT
WITH
LOWER
RIGHT
SHOULDER
AND HIP

INCORRECT

CORRECT

INCORRECT

UNEVENLY
BALANCED
CURVED
TO THE
LEFT

STRAIGHT
AND
EVENLY
BALANCED

UNEVENLY
BALANCED
CURVED
TO THE
RIGHT

INCORRECT

CORRECT

INCORRECT

Origin of many common postural faults

Longeing the Horse

Warning

Unless care and consideration is given to gait content, gait speed, and gait proportion with the way the horse posturally carries himself, more harm than good can result by incorrect, and/or improper longeing of the horse.

Work on the longe

Circle size 20 metres diameter. Maximum 45 minutes with a fit horse. There are a number of reasons for longeing and these are summarised below.

General—mental and physical To establish harmony, obedience, and co-ordination to produce an active and willing horse.

Improve the quality of the gaits To establish pleasant, active tempos at all three gaits, walk, trot, and canter.
• Walk Free stepping and developing overtracking.
• Trot Free, active, regular rhythmical diagonals.
• Canter Flowing, easy, free rhythmical strides.
• Transitions Upwards and downward—smooth, forward stretching, and definite. This is a most valuable exercise without the hindrance and weight of the rider.

Correct horse's postural faults Encourage correct head and neck carriage. Correct any tendency to lean, and/or tilt when moving on the longe, and to improve the suppleness of the horse's spine.

Improve equine efficiency/musculature To ensure that when moving on the left and right circles the horse is encouraged to improve the balance of the less good side. This includes the careful observation of all four limbs at each gait when circling to the left and right.

Remedial work on the longe To improve gait irregularities, and to correct specific physical weaknesses, and abnormalities. These if not corrected may result in excessive stress and tension, which may have been caused by earlier veterinary and/or riding problems. To use the gaits in a physio-therapeutical manner to strengthen weak, neglected, and/or other impoverished musculature.

Exercise on the longe

It would appear that 'exercising' a horse on the longe is something entirely different to normal longe work. This is not true, if such longeing is carried out in any old slipshod manner—spinning the horse round on the line—it will not be long before the horse will develop gait and postural faults. Longeing for exercise purposes must be carried out with the same meticulous care as normal correct gymnastic longeing. The object and aim being to improve all the qualities of the horse—not to try to destroy them.

Use of side-reins

In the early stages of longeing the horse—whether a young or older horse—the side-reins should be fitted long enough—equal on both reins—so that they do not restrict the forward movement of the horse in any way whatsoever. They should be long enough to allow the horse to carry his head at about 45 degrees and his neck stretched parallel to the ground at wither height. When the horse moves correctly in this way at walk, trot and canter, they can be shortened equally—two holes at a time approximately every two weeks, till the horse accepts the bit, and carries himself in a light and efficient manner. Do not overbend the horse.

'. . . If you are reasonably well placed in an equestrian competition, do not forget it was the horse who made it possible . . .'

Aims and objectives of longeing the horse:

1 To equalise lateral balance
2 To equalise lateral flexibility
3 To develop a convex outline
4 To improve gait quality
5 To strengthen musculature
6 To improve limb flexion in preparation for weight carrying

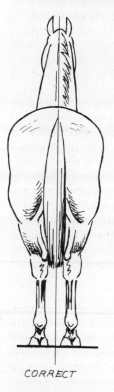

CORRECT

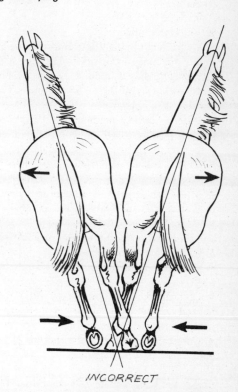

INCORRECT

When longeing the horse it is essential that the horse is encouraged to move upright. If the horse is allowed to develop—or is encouraged—to lean and/or tilt inward or outward when being worked on the longe this will create a number of problems which are not easy to see and recognise. The first one is that the horse has to stiffen his spine to maintain his balance. The second is that he must increase his speed the greater the tilt or lean. The third is having to carry his head and neck to the outside to support himself against the pull(s) on the longe. Finally, any or all of these problems tend to stiffen at least one pair of lateral limbs and can lead to irregular locomotion, i.e. dishing or plaiting. No longe lesson should be carried out for more than 45 minutes unless there is a particular reason and the trainer is fully aware of the possible physical consequences

Longeing the Rider

Warning
Unless due care is given to gait content, gait speed, and gait proportion, in accordance with the rider's physical fitness and experience, permanent injury and much harm can result from bad, and/or incorrect longeing.

Work on the longe
The aims and objects are to improve the all round qualities of the rider—the length of each stage is based upon five longe lessons each week of app 20 to 30 minutes. The purpose is to improve:
- Rider's poise, maintaining controlled vertical posture in all gaits and transitions . . .
- Rider's balance, controlled suppleness in the vertical plane . . .
- Minimum tension, maintaining balance by seat contact and body weight alone . . .
- Use of body weight, and seat to produce as and when required the various applications of the bracing of the back . . .
- Independent use of the limbs—hands and legs . . .
- Co-ordinating all the body aids, i.e., natural aids, with the maximum of effectiveness and the minimum of force . . .
- Correct absorption of the motion of the gaits . . .

Stage 1 Approximately 3 months. The gentle bracing of the back to achieve a balanced, efficient, perpendicular body posture with the minimum of stress and tension. This stage has to be carried out with much care and common-sense by the teacher/instructor being under-demanding rather than over-demanding.

Stage 2 Approximately 3 months. Bracing the back to push forward on a parallel plane—strengthening all muscles from seat to waist. This stage is the normal follow-up to Stage 1, from which the pupil/rider should find the physical effort reasonably easy, when practised in holding the gaits, and leading into the various transitions—upward and downward.

Stage 3 Approximately 3 months. Bracing the back downward and forward at one and the same time. This is best achieved and felt by the rider pressing his 'folded arms behind his back' downward and forward against his loins, the rider adjusting the tension as required.

Stage 4 Appproximately 3 months. Bracing the back to push/urge and lift upward and forward at one and the same time. This is achieved by correct thigh control, i.e., giving the impression of the rider trying to lift the saddle upward and forward with the thighs playing a predominant role, aided by the seat and loins.

Seldom is a good lesson ever witnessed, because few, if any teachers have had the necessary experience in the quality—and quantity—of correct work on the longe. What usually happens is that in their enthusiasm, teachers/instructors usually slacken and loosen the rider's musculature, which in turn weakens—instead of improving the seat. Teaching the rider on the longe is, first, a science, which progresses as an art. From a balanced posture/seat the rider refines his applications which develop aesthetic qualities.

'. . . There is no figure and/or exercise in the dressage curriculum which encourages a horse to flex his limbs and use his brain as required in sensible jumping . . .'

Aims and objectives of riding on the longe:

1 To improve balance
2 To develop poise
3 To reduce excess tension
4 To develop independent limb use
5 To master braced-back applications

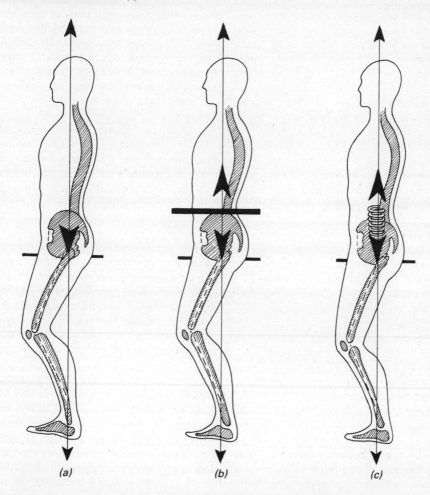

(a)   (b)   (c)

The basic phases—Stage 1: learning to sit correctly when on the longe:
(a) While remaining still and upright the rider must learn to sit deep, remaining supple in the loins, and without in any way tightening the buttocks so that the full seat and the thighs are in 'adhesive' contact with the largest possible area of the saddle.

(b) Having mastered the still upright posture with a deep full contact seat, the rider has now to learn that phase of body control, where—without in any way 'lightening the seat', the body above the waist has to be lifted/eased/stretched upward, i.e. above the waist the rider must grow taller.

(c) The next and final task is to learn loin suppleness and loin control, with the action simulating a coiled spring in lieu of the lumbar vertebrae. With supple buttocks and the thighs maintaining full contact with the saddle, the rider is now in an excellent position to fully absorb the movement and action of the horse, in the gait transitions and the gait variants, without any part of the body becoming stiff and/or tight

Glossary
of
Equine Locomotion

'. . . A little research should occupy every spare moment in the understanding of the science and art of horsemanship . . .'

The terms/words given here are briefly defined in a way to give information about the things for which they stand. They are based upon the correct theory and practice of classical equitation and presented as an aid to equestrian scholarship.

GAIT — A particular mode or manner used by the horse in locomotion, e.g., walk, trot, pace, canter, and gallop. Each gait is sub-divided into many and various arbitrary categories.

STEP — The completed action of the raising, and replacing on the ground, of a single foot; or, two feet when they are put on the ground at one and the same time, as in trot and pace, and one step in canter stride.

STRIDE — One completed action of the raising, and replacing on the ground, of all four feet.

PHASE — A particular instant during the act of locomotion.

LOCOMOTION — Moving from place to place. The displacement of the centre of gravity while maintaining equilibrium.

WALK — Four steps to each stride; evenly spaced, always with at least two feet on the ground. Can commence with any limb in this recurring sequence, left hind/left fore/right hind/right fore.

TROT — Two steps to each stride; alternate diagonal support.

PACE — Two steps to each stride; alternate lateral support.

CANTER — Three steps to each stride; hind foot/diagonal support/fore foot.

GALLOP — Four steps to each stride:
Transverse Gallop: left hind/right hind—left fore/right fore—or—right hind/left hind—right fore/left fore.
Rotary Gallop: left hind/right hind/right fore/ left fore—or—right hind/left hind/left fore/right fore.

RHYTHM — Time/stress factor of each footfall, or step, in a complete stride, i.e.,
a) the length of time the foot is in contact with the ground . . .
b) the stress, or pressure with which the foot is placed on the ground . . .
e.g., a skittish and excited horse usually

'jumps' or 'hops' around with his feet touching the ground for only a moment, with the lightest pressure, and minimum contact. A tired horse, finds it difficult to lift his feet from the ground, hence maximum pressure/contact on the ground for much longer and indefinite periods of time.

Examples of correct and incorrect walk rhythm, where each stride consists of four steps:

Correct (Normal)—1, 2, 3, 4, 1, 2, 3, 4, 1, 2, 3, 4, etc.

The 'time' is regular throughout.

The 'stress' is regular throughout.

Incorrect (Abnormal)—1, 2, 3, hop, 1, 2, 3, hop, 1, 2, 3, hop, etc.

The 'time' is irregular to the correct normal walk, but it is regular in this incorrect sequence.

The 'stress' is irregular to the correct normal walk, but it is regular in this incorrect sequence.

Summary—At a walk, a lame horse can have good rhythm (each stride following the same sequence/pattern), but it is not the correct walk rhythm of a healthy horse.

CADENCE   The sequence of placing the feet on the ground, i.e., the steps in each stride. For example, when a horse trots, it is assumed that he puts both diagonal feet on the ground at one and the same time, i.e., two steps to each stride.

This would be ideal, but is seldom ever carried out correctly. Usually there are two separate footfalls, in quick succession, often with only one diagonal pair of limbs, but sometimes with both diagonal pairs of limbs. When there are two separate footfalls in one, or both diagonal pairs of limbs, the cadence would be incorrect.

TEMPO   Speed—mph/kph.

Note   The keen equestrian will enhance their scholarship and appreciation by researching the various 'loose' terminology used in horsemanship by consulting the many relevant dictionaries, e.g., physics, mechanics, music and ballet, etc.